YOU'RE PROBABLY GAYISH

of related interest

Gay Man Talking
All the Conversations We Never Had
Daniel Harding
ISBN 978 1 83997 094 8
eISBN 978 1 83997 095 5

Sounds Fake But Okay
An Asexual and Aromantic Perspective on Love, Relationships,
Sex, and Pretty Much Anything Else
Sarah Costello and Kayla Kaszyca
ISBN 978 1 83997 001 6
eISBN 978 1 83997 002 3

How to Understand Your Sexuality
A Practical Guide for Exploring Who You Are
Meg-John Barker and Alex Iantaffi
Illustrated by Jules Scheele
Foreword by Erika Moen
ISBN 978 1 78775 618 2
eISBN 978 1 78775 619 9

You're Probably Gayish

The Truth (and Lies) Behind 17 Gay Stereotypes

Mike Johnson & Kyle Getz

Foreword by Davey Wavey

Jessica Kingsley Publishers
London and Philadelphia

First published in Great Britain in 2025 by Jessica Kingsley Publishers
An imprint of John Murray Press

1

Copyright © Mike Johnson and Kyle Getz 2025
Foreword Copyright © Davey Wavey 2025

Front cover image source: Shutterstock®

**This book contains mention of homophobia, transphobia,
substance abuse, and child abuse.**

A CIP catalogue record for this title is available from the
British Library and the Library of Congress

ISBN 978 1 80501 124 8
eISBN 978 1 80501 125 5

Printed and bound in Great Britain by Clays Ltd

Jessica Kingsley Publishers' policy is to use papers that are natural,
renewable, and recyclable products and made from wood grown in
sustainable forests. The logging and manufacturing processes are expected
to conform to the environmental regulations of the country of origin.

Jessica Kingsley Publishers
Carmelite House
50 Victoria Embankment
London EC4Y 0DZ

www.jkp.com

John Murray Press
Part of Hodder & Stoughton Limited
An Hachette UK Company

The authorised representative in the EEA is Hachette Ireland,
8 Castlecourt Centre, Dublin 15, D15 XTP3, Ireland (email: info@hbgi.ie)

Contents

Foreword by Davey Wavey   7

Acknowledgments   10

Preface: *How Gayish Are You?*   11

Quiz!   **14**

1: You're Probably Crazy   19

2: You're Probably an Only Child   31

3: You Probably Have a Piercing in Your Right Ear   41

4: You Probably Have Limp Wrists   51

5: You're Probably Hot and Jacked   61

6: You Probably Had a 4.0 GPA   73

7: You Probably Have Impeccable Taste   83

8: You're Probably a Pedophile   93

9: You Probably Watch *The Golden Girls*   101

10: You're Probably a Flight Attendant, Hairdresser, or Nurse 103

11:   You've Probably Never Touched a Vagina   113

12:   You Probably Love Pop Divas   121

13:   You Probably Love Musicals   131

14:   You Probably Have Good Gaydar   139

15:   You're Probably a Slut   149

16:   You Probably Get Drunk and High   159

17:   You Probably Love Iced Coffee   169

Scoring Your Quiz   **179**

Conclusion:*You're Probably Gayish*   *181*

Endnotes   *185*

Foreword

By Davey Wavey

Years ago, I was being interviewed about my YouTube channel. For nearly two decades, I've been making videos about sex and sexuality for gay men. From anal douching tutorials to straight guys trying prostate stimulators to masturbation stroke techniques, truly nothing is sacred. And with nearly a billion video views and counting, I've seemingly reached some percentage of our community. Or at least one committed fan who is playing my videos on repeat. Thanks, Mom?

The interviewer—who was another gay man, I might add—somewhat pointedly asked, "But aren't you concerned that you're reinforcing negative stereotypes about gay men? After all, it *is* a stereotype that gay men are sex-obsessed and feminine."

There's a lot to unpack in that question. Including a handful of assumptions—like that sex or femininity are *negative*—and a decent dose of internalized homophobia. But let's try.

To be fair, my YouTube channel *is* about sex. But does that make me sex-obsessed? I began to wonder about other niche YouTubers like those who make videos about Lego. Are they brick-obsessed? Or just creating on-brand content for topics about which they're passionate. Not knowing of any 12-step Lego programs, I'd suggest the latter.

I talk about sex because someone needs to. Sex education is an abject failure in this country. And most parents are equally clueless about sex—especially queer sex—and lack the vocabulary to teach their children anything meaningful.

My anal douching tutorials, for example, have been viewed millions of times, and an entire generation of bottoms (and tops) are enjoying the fruits of this shared wisdom. And though this information is important for good and fulfilling sex, it's probably not a topic most parents or schools would consider covering. And that's where my YouTube videos come in. It's a thankless job with no statues, monuments, or parades, but I'm happy to be an unsung hero of our movement.

So, am I sex-obsessed? Or just passionate about giving people information to connect with their bodies, their pleasure, and their partners?

And sure, I'm feminine. My voice is higher than most and I can't open my mouth without also waving my hands. But is femininity in men negative? Hello, internalized homophobia. In a world riddled with toxic masculinity, I'd suggest that men who embody feminine traits are modeling a more sustainable version of manhood. One that this world desperately needs if we have any hope of survival. Like many gay men, I embody some stereotypes. Beyond the so-called sex obsession and the admitted hand waving, I spend a lot of time in the gym and have a sculpted body. Perhaps most stereotypical of all, I was a college cheerleader for a Catholic university that actively discriminated against me. It doesn't get gayer than that.

But, on the other hand, I also break gay stereotypes. I've never had a sip of alcohol. I live in a cabin with a wood stove. I don't go to circuit parties. And I only recently tried poppers. Admittedly, this list is quite short and now I wonder if someone else should have written this introduction. Well, too late now.

I asked the interviewer if he'd rather me talk about football scores. Or civil war reenactments. Or maybe sectional couches, because straight people like those, right? Though I have no interest in these topics and find sectional couches to be a crime against humanity, I'd certainly break gay stereotypes.

The interview never aired, needless to say.

Here's what I know: it's not our job to break stereotypes. It's not my job. And it's certainly not yours.

It's also not our job to be just like straight people. Straight people ought to celebrate and love us *not* because we're just like them, but simply because we're people, too. For me, the argument of "give us rights because we're just like you" misses the point. Indeed, as queers, we *are* different. And those differences are beautiful and have proven to benefit society in some amazing ways over the millennia. Imagine if a straight person painted the Sistine Chapel? No, thanks.

However, it *is* our job to be ourselves. We don't get much time on this floating rock called Earth. In fact, each of us has won the cosmic lottery just to exist. So to squander that precious time being anything other than ourselves talking about sectional couches seems particularly preposterous.

In this journey of life, you will reinforce some stereotypes, and you'll shatter others. But none of that really matters. What *does* matter is authenticity. And authenticity is a goal to which all of us ought to aspire. In our pursuit of authenticity, we'll face many demons, challenges, shame, and internalized homophobia. It's not an easy journey, but it is fucking worth it.

Here's to leaning into authenticity—and whatever stereotypes you embody or break along the way.

Acknowledgments

There are so many people that have made *Gayish* the show it is today. Thank you to our producers, Fucking Dan and Derek Tellin. Thank you to all the guests who have been gracious enough to join the show, especially Patty Johnson, aka Ma Johnson, aka Mike's mom, who is one of our most frequent. Thank you to Davey Wavey for being such a strong supporter of ours and for agreeing to write the Foreword to this book. Thank you to all the other LGBTQ+ podcasts for the countless hours and all the dedication you put into your show (and especially those we've been lucky enough to appear as guests on). And thank you to all our loyal listeners that are part of the Gayish Agenda. Your support means the world to us, and we hope we've helped make your lives a little more *Gayish*.

Preface
How Gayish Are You?

We're here to bridge the gap between sexuality and actuality. And we're also here to write a book. The whole experience is surreal. The path we took to get to this point has taken the better part of 15 years. When we met in 2008, we both worked for Microsoft, met as colleagues at a gay employee resource group event, and have been friends ever since. *Just* friends, by the way. We've seen each other go through so much life in that time. We've watched each other date, find boyfriends, move in, have fights, break up, move out, get married, get divorced, have surgery, struggle with mental health, gain weight, lose weight, have STIs, change jobs, be unemployed, do yoga, drink too much, do drugs, deal with sick parents, go to funerals, stay up late watching YouTube, sleep too much, have insomnia, change medications, worry about money, make questionable fashion choices, struggle to select furniture, install light fixtures, endure brain magnets, host parties, be absolute sluts, tip go-go boys, laugh until it hurt, fuck up cooking dinner, write songs, make movies, play video games, and lie to ourselves. If friendship means showing up, we've done it for sure.

In the spring of 2017, we had the bright idea to start a podcast. We had worked on creative projects in the past together, primarily digital shorts Kyle would write and Mike would help with. So, when we sat down to think of ways that we could work together creatively on a project, one of us (and we're not sure which) suggested a podcast. We gave it a shot. We talked a lot about wanting to explore gay stereotypes and to really send out the message that, although we might have the image of what a gay man is in our imaginations, there's no wrong way to be a gay man. Neither of us have felt like we 100% fit into gay culture, and we wanted everyone like us to know that that's OK.

We came up with a basic structure and bought one shitty microphone.* We connected the mic to Kyle's laptop, pushed record, Mike said, "Hello everyone** in the podcast universe, this is *Gayish,*" and coming up on 400 episodes later, the rest is history. *Gayish* was born.

Early on doing the show, we talked about how happy we would be if we somehow got 50 people to listen to our content. When we started having 100 people listen regularly, and then 1000, it really started to feel like we were part of something important. It still does.

Through these seven years of doing the show, we've talked about a bunch of stereotypes. Some of them have been surprising, others silly, and yet others heavy. Slowly but surely, a little community built up around the show, and we realized that we had something to say that people were responding to. Watching that weird little family form has been one of the greatest joys of doing the podcast.

In talking about where to take our ideas next, one logical step seemed to be to write about it. Well, a logical step to Kyle at least; he's a writer. Mike was terrified. We pitched an idea to one publisher, who agreed to start developing a book with us but then he dropped us like a bad habit when he discovered we have an episode called

---

* For episode 2 we forgot to plug it in.
** Actually, Mike said, "Hello every*body* in the podcast universe," the only episode for which that is true and quite the piece of *Gayish* trivia to know.

Felching*** in our catalog. Eventually we found a publisher that had not only listened to us but wanted to put more queer content out in the world and liked our message and our vibe. We're extremely grateful for that.

In this book, we've tried to stick to our core values, irreverent approach, and commitment to our basic message that we're all a little Gayish. Even straight people. At the front of the book is a (light-hearted) quiz measuring just how Gayish you are. However, we want to make it clear that this book, and the quiz, is from the gay male perspective. While we talk about all parts of the LGBTQ+ rainbow on Gayish, and we love our straight allies, and we love being allies to the queer sub-communities we aren't a part of, we realized early on when writing this book that we couldn't do this project justice if we tried to write all of the things for all of the people.

We also want to make it clear that we are not doctors, psychologists, social workers, researchers, or scientists. We are just two schmoes that started a podcast. We've learned a lot about this stuff along the way, but not enough to qualify as experts of any kind. While we try to be accurate as much as possible, we've probably fucked something up. Let's be real, we've almost certainly fucked up multiple somethings. As the McElroy Brothers say at the beginning of MBMBAM, "their advice should never be followed." Ditto for us.

The point here is to have a little tongue-in-cheek fun (slightly less fun than tongue-between-cheek fun) and explore some very real stereotypes about gay men and their impact. Thank you for reading, and thank you for listening. Thank you for the opportunity to bring a little bit of our friendship and our message into your brains.

. . . .

*** Episode 239.

QUIZ HOW GAYISH ARE YOU?

First, take this quiz below, picking the answer that most closely fits for you. Then, as you read the book, we'll show you how to score your answers. (Each question will be answered in the chapter of the same number.)

1. Are you taking medication for a diagnosed mental illness?
   a. Yes
   b. No
   c. No, but I should be
   d. No, I'm taking medication for fun!

2. How many older brothers do you have?
   a. 0
   b. 1
   c. 2
   d. 3+

3. Is your right ear pierced?
   a. No
   b. Yes, and I know it's the gay ear
   c. Yes, and so is the left ear

4. Has anyone ever described your movements as "swishy"?
   a. Yes, and I fixed that shit
   b. Yes, and this is who I am, goddammit
   c. No, why would they?
   d. No, my feet don't move when I dance

5. How would you describe your torso?
   a. 6 pack
   b. 8 pack
   c. Half rack

6. What was your high school GPA?
   a. 4.0, I'm brilliant
   b. 3.0–3.9
   c. < 3.0, not an academic powerhouse
   d. 2.5, but I sucked a lot of dicks

7. Where is your furniture from?
   a. Pottery Barn, Crate & Barrel, and West Elm
   b. Target, Ikea, and the thrift shop
   c. Wal-Mart, Craigslist, and from when my brother
      moved out

8. Are you a threat to children?
   a. Yes, I am
   b. Yes, but just the altar boys
   c. Yes, but only if they ruin my flight to Palm Springs
   d. No

9. How many episodes of *The Golden Girls* have you
   watched?
   a. 0
   b. 1–4
   c. 5–179
   d. All 180 and *The Golden Palace*, too

10. What's your profession?
    a. Flight attendant

   b. Nurse

   c. Hairdresser

   d. None of the above, but something equally gay

   e. None of the above

11. What metal is your gay star made from?

   a. Silver

   b. Gold

   c. Platinum

   d. Lead

12. Which concert would you choose first?

   a. Cher opening for Madonna

   b. Maroon 5 opening for Usher

   c. Metallica opening for Bruce Springsteen

   d. Country

13. Who starred as Fanny Brice in Funny Girl?

   a. Barbra Streisand

   b. Lea Michele

   c. Janeane Garofalo

   d. Isn't Fanny the British word for vagina?

14. Were you surprised when Anderson Cooper came out?

   a. Yes, he seemed so butch!

   b. No, I knew the whole time

   c. What? He's gay?!?

15. What's your "body count"?

   a. 0–15

   b. Over 15

   c. Over 1000, with 3 zeroes

16. Did you get drunk and/or do drugs last month?
    a. Got drunk only
    b. Did drugs only
    c. Got drunk and did drugs
    d. None of the above

17. How often do you drink iced coffee?
    a. Never
    b. Sometimes
    c. Every day and twice on Sundays
    d. Only when Taylor the latte boy is working

1

You're Probably Crazy

What's the stereotype?

Gay people are mentally ill.

Do people really believe that?

Yup. Historically, being gay has been considered a mental illness by even the most reputable of medical organizations. As (straight) people try to find explanations for why some people are gay, mental illness has been a common go-to. Even today, you'll still hear some anti-LGBTQ+ conservatives use this stereotype as a way to denigrate and other our community.

Kyle, are you the crazy one?

I came out to my parents when I was in college, but I had been stressing over my gayness since I was in junior high. Back in those days, I didn't realize I was "discovering my sexuality." I didn't think of it in those terms. I just thought Daniel was cute. Daniel and I ran cross country together, but he was a year older and much faster than me. Unfortunately, I could never catch Daniel. I thought about him a lot, usually late at night. Oh, Daniel. *cue wistful music* *Oh, Daniel.*

I liked boys. I didn't try to. I didn't mean to. I just did. And as a kid in 8th grade in the late 90s, I already knew that being gay was a bad thing. In school, I was only bullied a little. I was told I was going to hell, not because I was gay, but because I wasn't Christian. Still, I had heard enough gay jokes and comments and insults that I knew to keep it to myself.

I waited and waited and waited for it to go away. I prayed to a god I didn't really believe in to take it away. I didn't want to be gay. But it didn't go anywhere. It didn't change. I kept liking boys. Unfortunately, it wasn't a phase. My sophomore year of college was when I finally accepted that it was here to stay. I had felt it since junior high, and it's just who I am. I came out to my parents after that. It didn't go well.

My parents and I fought and cried a lot after I came out. They had a hard time with it. I'm lucky that they still told me they loved me unconditionally, and they didn't kick me out or cut me off. But that didn't mean they liked it. Unlike most kids that grew up in the suburbs of Texas, it wasn't about religion. Our family was never religious. But no one is immune to the norms religion inflicts on society. They thought being gay was wrong. They thought I was wrong.

They told me they wanted me to go to therapy. I don't remember them telling me exactly why, but the understanding was that I needed professional help to fix me. It was hard knowing that my parents thought I was broken just because of who I was and who I liked. That there was something inside of me they thought wasn't right. Then again, I had felt a deep sadness for as long as I could remember. I had once called it the "dark clouds" in a bad poem I wrote when I was younger. Maybe they were right. Maybe there really was something wrong with me. Maybe I *was* crazy.

But where did the idea that being gay means you're crazy come from?

My parents weren't the first people to believe that being gay meant something was wrong. In fact, at the time that I came out to them, being gay was still included in the DSM, aka the *Diagnostic and Statistical Manual of Mental Disorders,* aka the Bible of mental health disorders. So, according to the best information available to them at the time, I *did* need therapy. I tried to explain what I knew inside: I was gay and there was nothing I could do about it. But my message wasn't getting through. It turns out, I wasn't the first person to try to argue this point either.

As I read about where the idea that gay people are crazy came from, the one work that came up most often was an influential book called *Psychopathia Sexualis,* which was written in 1886 by this German psychiatrist dude named Richard von Krafft-Ebing. Hold on to that fact in case you ever need to impress your gay friends at a party. He was influenced by Darwinian theory, which said that anything sexual that doesn't lead to a baby (like gay stuff or masturbation) is wrong. He believed that gayness was a hereditary degenerative disorder. Fuck you, Krafft-Ebing. Then again, part of his theory was a revelation because it was, as one modern psychiatrist called it, "an ironic twist of the modern 'born gay' theory." He did, in fact, think people were born that way. He just also thought it was a disorder.

That modern psychiatrist is Dr. Jack Drescher, a psychiatrist and psychoanalyst, formerly the Clinical Professor of Psychiatry at Columbia University (i.e. very, very smart). He wrote the paper "Out of DSM: Depathologizing homosexuality."[1] McSmarty said there have been three theories on what gayness is: a disease, a phase, or a normal variation. Obvs the last one is the correct one, and don't let anyone tell you any different. (My words, not McSmarty's.)

Although the ideas in *Psychopathia Sexualis* were the ones that caught on, that being gay was a disease, there were plenty of activists and smart people out there explaining that being gay was normal. For example, there's Karl Heinrich Ulrichs. He was a German writer and lawyer who could be considered the first modern gay activist. In 1867, he argued against the German anti-homosexuality laws in what Wikipedia called "possibly the first instance of a sexually modern 'coming out'." (Yes, I'm using Wikipedia for this. Deal with it.) Born in 1825, he used the word "urning" to describe himself since the word "homosexual" hadn't been invented yet.

Mike: *Sometimes a cigar is just a cigar, Kyle.*

Kyle: *But sometimes it's in my ass.*

EPISODE 119: THERAPY

Another influential person was Karl Mária Kertbeny, a Hungarian journalist and human rights activist, who coined the word "homosexual" in a letter to Ulrichs. I think it's cute that they knew each other, and I like to imagine they were BFFs, but that's based on literally nothing but my imagination. Kertbeny believed being gay was completely natural, too, and argued against sodomy laws. It's sad, but somehow telling, that the word "homosexual" became popularized, not by way of the human rights activist who created it, but rather by Krafft-Ebing, who used it in *Psychopathia Sexualis* where he called us degenerates.

The most famous psychoanalyst of all time, Sigmund Freud, also had theories on gay people. He believed everyone started out bisexual, and they just grew out of it to become straight. (Side note: if you believe that everyone is a little bisexual, you're probably bisexual.) Therefore, Freud believed, being gay came from a sort of inability to move past this phase. I know Freud was wrong about a lot. Sometimes he's just a dick. But this was actually a pretty progressive view for the time.

When Freud had gay patients and couldn't change their orientation, he came to accept that homosexuality was innate. Near the end of his life in 1935, a mother wrote to him asking to help her gay son. In his now-infamous response, Freud said, "It is nothing to be ashamed of, no vice, no degradation; it cannot be classified as an illness; we consider it to be a variation of the sexual function, produced by a certain arrest of sexual development." He also explained to her that, if her son struggles with other mental health issues, treatment can help with *those* issues, not the gayness: "If he is unhappy, neurotic, torn by conflicts, inhibited in his social life, analysis may bring him harmony, peace of mind, full efficiency, whether he remains homosexual or gets changed."[2] No, it's not a perfect statement in support of gay people, but at least he didn't view it as a disease like Krafft-Ebing. Fuck you again, Krafft-Ebing.

Unfortunately, Freud's views of homosexuality weren't what caught on. Instead, it was those of Sandor Rado, a Hungarian psychoanalyst, who disputed Freud, suggested gayness was pathological, and indicated it could be treated (i.e. changed). In fact, psychoanalysts played a big role in the spread of misinformation about homosexuality because their theories were often based on their own patients, which is an unfair sample because they're made up of people who are already seeking treatment. It would be like going to a beach and asking who's been sunburned. That's bad because of... the scientific method? I don't know. I just know it's bad technique. Among those psychoanalysts was Dr. Charles Socarides, who believed gayness was caused by distant fathers and overbearing mothers. Fuck you too, Socarides.

It got better eventually though, right?

The view of homosexuality as a mental illness was solidified in 1952 when the first edition of the DSM came out and listed homosexuality as a "sociopathic personality disturbance" along with "transvestism, pedophilia, fetishism and sexual sadism." The American Psychiatric Association, the organization that publishes the DSM, re-upped their homophobia in 1968 when the second edition reclassified homosexuality under "sexual deviation." I think the DSM is a product of the beliefs at the time, that gayness was a disease. It didn't create that view, but it could influence others, especially psychiatrists and other medical professionals, to take that view given its intent is to show the best scientific evidence available.

Luckily, there were some researchers that had dissenting (and dare I say, correct) thoughts on the matter. In the 1950s, a psychologist named Evelyn Hooker did important (and scientifically sound) research where she compared 30 gay men, none of whom were psychiatric patients, with a control group of 30 straight men and didn't find any psychological disturbances. This was important as it countered the common narrative that gay people were all disturbed.

Another well-known researcher is sexologist Dr. Alfred Kinsey, who's famous for the Kinsey scale, a rudimentary understanding of sexuality that rates it on a scale from 0 to 6, from exclusively heterosexual to exclusively homosexual. Turns out, human sexuality isn't as easy as a 0–6 scale, but again, it was progressive for the time. In 1948, he estimated that 10% of the population was gay, which surprised people at the time because they didn't realize that near that many people were gay. (Today's estimates put the percentage of LGBTQ+ people in the population anywhere from 7–21%.) When researchers broaden their study to the general gay population, they find that gay people are kinda... normal. Go figure.

Gay activists also pushed back against the DSM's designation as "sociopathic" or "deviant." Not only was it wrong and hurtful, but the fact that it was listed as a mental illness meant gay people could be sent to conversion therapy, institutionalized, or even lobotomized, just because they were gay. (We now know, based on evidence, that no one can change your sexual orientation, and discredited techniques like conversion therapy can cause a variety of issues including depression and suicide attempts.) So, gay activists stormed the 1970 and 1971 American Psychiatric Association annual conferences, pushing the organization to change the DSM. Other activists, like Frank Kameny and Barbara Gittings, sat on panels at those same conferences to allow attendees to hear directly from a gay person, some for the first time.

But the most influential person in this space is arguably Dr. John Fryer. He was a gay psychiatrist, and he stood in front of his peers at the annual conference in 1972 and stated, "I am a homosexual. I am a psychiatrist." A brave move, even though he wore a Nixon mask and a wig, distorted his voice, and went by Dr. H. Anonymous, so worried was he about his professional reputation. (New Halloween costume idea!) He was among the Gay-P-A, a gay psychiatrists' organization, and the only one from that organization willing to stand in front of his peers and prove that gay psychiatrists existed. The gay is calling from inside the house!

Because of those efforts, in 1973, there was a change. Homosexuality wasn't removed completely, but the American Psychiatric Association *did* remove homosexuality as a mental illness. As a compromise, they replaced it with "sexual orientation disturbance," which meant that homosexuality was an illness only if the person was "disturbed by, in conflict with, or wished to change their sexual orientation." But then again, who wouldn't be disturbed while being gay? If I can be lobotomized just for being gay, of course I'm gonna be disturbed! The threat of violence is disturbing! Although the update wasn't perfect (a recurring theme in activism), it was a major step forward. It meant gayness itself was no longer pathologized. I don't think everyone in the US was reading the DSM like it was Dickens, but progress among the scientific community is one pathway to full LGBTQ+ acceptance.

Revising the DSM in 1973 was important, but it alone also

couldn't immediately revise public consciousness. My grandparents and my parents both grew up in a world that told them being gay was wrong or could be changed. It's no surprise then, that my parents wanted me to go to therapy to therapize the gay out of me. One of the best ironies of my gay life is that I did, in fact, sign up for therapy through my college, and I was assigned to a graduate student who, as it turns out, was also gay. I had already come to accept that my gay wasn't going away, and he had no intention of trying to change me. Instead, I used my time in therapy to talk about the struggles of my scarred relationship with my parents—and my depression.

Did therapy help?

My first year at college was rough. I was well prepared for the academic challenges, but I also felt numb to it all. I didn't know if it was because I didn't have many friends at first or because I was in a new city for the first time in my life or because—well, I just didn't know. I spent a lot of time sleeping and watching DVDs of *Family Guy*. I skipped classes, even when they were at 12:30pm. I complained to all my high school friends who visited that I wasn't happy. Whatever dark clouds had been rolling up throughout my high school experience were here, and they weren't going away.

Since then, I've continued to struggle with depression to the point that I haven't been able to get out of bed at times. I've had lasting suicidal ideation and thoughts that could take me down spirals. I've cut myself in an attempt to stop the pain. Dealing with depression is fucking horrible. There's no other way to say it. Not only have I had to deal with the depression itself, but I've had to deal with it *while being depressed,* which means I constantly doubt that I actually have depression while simultaneously judging myself as being a bad person because I have it. It has made me feel weak, useless, and unimportant. And, because of the stigma around mental health, especially as a guy, sometimes society says that I'm right to think those things.

Sometimes I feel guilty that I have depression. I grew up in a loving household with a loving family and parents who are still married to this day. Even though coming out was a rough patch, my parents eventually came around and supported me to the point where I once brought a boyfriend home for Christmas. I've always had food on the table, a roof over my head, and friends beside me. So how am I allowed to be depressed? Why am I crazy? Is it because I'm gay?

As it turns out, depression doesn't need a reason. It can just be. It's frustrating, but then again, so are lots of medical diagnoses that feel unexpected and unfair. But maybe there is a reason, at least in my case. I grew up liking boys. I didn't even want to like boys! And still, because of it, I was trained that I needed to hide it and be ashamed of it. That I was wrong. That I needed fixing. I was constantly reminded that my interests and activities and even my very instincts were wrong because they were gay. Growing up learning to hate myself very well might have caused my depression.

According to the National Alliance on Mental Illness, lesbian, gay, and bisexual adults are more than twice as likely as straight people to struggle with mental health challenges like depression or anxiety. Transgender adults are four times as likely, compared to cisgender people.[3] As a result, we're at a higher risk for things like substance use, homelessness, and suicide.

Mike: *A lot of mental health is just putting one foot in front of the other, and sometimes you gotta turn around to realize that you've walked a while.*

EPISODE 119: THERAPY

No matter the reason, I have diagnosed major depressive disorder. I do what I can to manage it. I go to therapy. I've tried dozens of different medications. I've even gotten TMS, aka transcranial magnetic stimulation, where they pulsed magnets into my brain to stimulate it and help tear myself out of severe depression. I'm working on it, and I believe it's something I'll continue to work on for the rest of my life.

In 2013, homosexuality was completely removed from the DSM, but its damage has been done. Not just because of the DSM, but all of it: the bad science and the conservative religious beliefs and the unhealthy view of sex and the stigma and all the people who, without even talking to a gay person, condemned it as insanity. All that societal bullshit culminated to mean that little junior high me knew he was really into Daniel and also knew he couldn't say anything. It messed me up. Society messed me up. I do struggle with mental health. I joke that I'm crazy. But being gay didn't make me crazy. Homophobia did.

So, is the stereotype true?

Yes and no. Being gay in and of itself is not a mental illness, and it isn't borne of any psychological problems. Studies have shown, and the major medical organizations agree, that there is nothing wrong with being gay. It's normal, just uncommon. What's true is that, as a result of homophobia (including the kind that stems from being called mentally ill), gay people are more likely to have mental health issues, such as depression or anxiety. So, in a way, yes, gay people are more likely to be mentally ill.

What's the final verdict?

Misleading, but true.

SCORING YOUR QUIZ: QUESTION #1

In the quiz (page 14), we asked if you were taking medication for a diagnosed mental illness. Here's how to score your results:

a. Yes: 2 gay points (because gay people are, in fact, more likely to have a mental illness)
b. No: 0 gay points
c. No, but I should be: 1 gay point (because you don't need a diagnosis to need help)
d. No, I'm taking medication for fun!: 1 gay point (because gay people are more likely to do recreational drugs than straight people; see Chapter 16)

You're Probably
an Only Child

What's the stereotype?

If you're an only child, you're more likely to be gay.

Where does that idea come from?

This is a stereotype that pops up in the 1950s and 1960s as gay people became more visible and an increasingly hostile society started
looking for "causes" for this "problem." Only children, it was thought,
are somehow deficient and broken, with all kinds of potential negative outcomes including, gasp, becoming a homosexual.

Mike, you're gay, right? But you're not an only child!

I am indeed super gay, and I have two younger brothers. So, right out
of the gate, at the very least, this is a stereotype that doesn't fit for
me or is busted altogether. But this idea that the kind of family you
were raised in impacts your chance of being gay is a persistent one,
and not just the idea it's because you're an only child. Some say that
single parents are more likely to have gay kids. Some say that's only

true if it's a single mom. Some say that really big families are more likely to have queer kids, which just seems like a matter of percentages to me but whatevs. Some say that divorce causes gay kids. The concept that being an only child somehow makes you gay is the one we're focusing on here; I'm just showing that there are lots of crazy ideas about family makeup determining who you want to bang.

All of those familial theories, being an only child included, are founded on the behaviors and circumstances we were raised in. What our family unit was like, after we got out of the womb and into the world, is the focus. The queer rallying call "born this way" leads us to believe that none of those things should matter. Ask any LGBTQ+ person, and they'll tell you, "I didn't choose this." But does that mean we were born this way? We also didn't choose our family situation.

It was the Victorians (it's always them) who really got the ball rolling on the idea that only children sucked and therefore might suck dick. In Victorian society, it was a woman's duty to have children, and stopping at just one was seen as her body tragically betraying her at best and contemptible selfishness at worst.[4] Only children were considered spoiled, bossy, shy, selfish, inflexible, and odd. Know what another word for odd is? Queer. Only children, also called "singletons" were considered queer, and often in both senses of the word.

G. Stanley Hall was by all measures a titan of early psychology. He was the very first President of the American Psychological Association.[5] He was also a dickbag fuckface asshole.* He hated gay people as sexual deviants,[6] thought masturbation was evil, and believed in eugenics (the idea that we need more white people than black people by any means necessary, including murdering the black

---

* Our first annual Dickbag Fuckface Asshole award, as voted on by our listeners, was Ron DeSantis in 2023.

people, because white people are superior). Anyway, he once said, "being an only child is a disease in itself" and repeated Sigmund Freud's belief that being an only child caused "sexual identity problems" (i.e. gayyyyy).[7]

Back in the 1950s, American culture in suburbia really shifted to the Leave It to Beaver model. You know, a happy, straight married couple with two kids and a dog. That kind of bullshit. But with the rise of McCarthyism and the Lavender Scare (see Chapter 8), Americans of the time started asking themselves, "where are all these gays coming from?" Paranoia set in, and every deviation from the standard, happy, modern nuclear family was suddenly suspect. Society really started worrying that the queerness of only children meant *queerness.*

But aren't only children actually pretty terrible people?

Even though a lot of stereotypes about only children persist to this day, many studies have shown them to be complete horseshit. One researcher, University of Texas psychologist Toni Falbo, even thinks being an only child has benefits. Falbo analyzed 500 studies involving only children and concluded they are just as emotionally stable, generous, mature, and popular as kids with brothers or sisters, but also smarter, more driven, and better educated.[8] And are they straighter? Turns out yes, they are, but maybe not for the reasons you'd think.

We have to go back to the idea that queer people are "born this way." It's an excellent song, by the way. Mad props to Lady Gaga. It strikes directly at the friction between the lived truth of queer people (that their queerness was thrust upon them) and the conservative talking point that God makes no mistakes so therefore queer people must have chosen to be deviant. The song is also very catchy and easy to dance to. If you dance, that is; not everyone has that particular gay gene. Speaking of gay genes, we've been looking for one for a pretty long time, hoping to prove that being gay is genetic and therefore not a choice.

How genetics work is definitely something that popular science has led people to believe they understand when they very much don't. This was especially true in the early days of sequencing the human genome. In 1993, "A linkage between DNA markers on the X chromosome and male sexual orientation" was published by Dean Hamer.[9] There were other researchers involved, but this became known as the Hamer study. They had discovered some strong indications that male homosexuality is passed through the maternal line. People assigned male at birth typically get one X chromosome from their mother and one Y chromosome from their father. People assigned female at birth typically get an X chromosome from each parent. A gene on the X chromosome would go a long way to explain the maternal line phenomenon, so Hamer's team decided to look closely and see if they could figure it out.

> **Michael Zakar:** *When we were coming out, our mom said, "I wish you had cancer—at least that's curable."*
>
> EPISODE 314: TWINS
> (W/ THE ZAKAR TWINS)

They thought they hit paydirt. They found one specific spot on the X chromosome that really was different for these gays. The Hamer study indicated "a statistical confidence level of more than 99 percent that [...] male sexual orientation is genetically influenced."[10] The media went wild with it as the smoking gun that proved there was a gay gene. Stories of the discovery of the gay gene entered the zeitgeist. Queer outlets proclaimed science gave them the right to say, "I told you so." Christians raced to reconcile this new discovery with their dogma.

It is a fundamental tenet of science that any study be reproducible, however. If it's valid, we'll be able to try it again and get the same result. For all of the brouhaha surrounding it and the splash it made in the media, the Hamer study was not reproducible, despite multiple attempts. Scientists love to bitch at each other about this stuff, and although Hamer maintains there's something there, the scientific community has largely shunned his study as being just not good enough or repeatable enough to claim what it claims. By 1999 the journal *Science* published a study indicating that gayness is, at a minimum, polygenetic and likely requires a combination of genes.[11]

A quick shoutout to whoever decided to name the journal *Science*. What a ballsy name. While other journals cover niche specific things like the *Journal of Cosmetics, Dermatological Sciences and Applications* (an actual journal), these guys were like "fuck it, we're doing *all of science*."

Remember my original quote from the Hamer study? It was "a statistical confidence level of more than 99 percent that [...] male sexual orientation is genetically influenced." Whenever you see an ellipsis you should really ask yourself what is hiding in there. What they really said is "a statistical confidence level of more than 99 percent that *at least one subtype of* male sexual orientation is genetically influenced."

Valid study or not, Hamer never claimed that there was *the* gay gene and he found it. Just that he was pretty sure they had found at least *one* cause of *one* type of gay. There are multiple types of gay; remember that. Unfortunately, this tendency to overstate scientific claims is something the media excels at. To widely broadcast an incorrect interpretation of an irreproducible study is pretty much how science journalism rolls. Be careful what you read and believe, this book included. We like neat and tidy explanations, and the media likes to give them to us. Humans are not neat and tidy, especially when it comes to sexuality.

It's pretty easy to realize that "a gay gene," much less "*the* gay gene" living on the X chromosome, isn't and can't be a slam dunk. Research on identical twins (meaning they have exactly the same X chromosome) has shown that if one is gay, there's a big chance the other one is too, but that chance is not 100%. There's no genetic light switch that switches on and suddenly makes you love Cher.[12]

In 2019, in the (again, very audaciously named) journal *Science,* a massive study was published basically saying there are no genes that immediately make someone gay, but there are a lot of genes that might *help* make someone gay, and that "it's effectively impossible to predict an individual's sexual behavior from their genome." That quote is Ben Neale, a geneticist at Massachusetts General Hospital and the Broad Institute who led the study. He also said, "Genetics is less than half of this story for sexual behavior."[13]

So, what is the other half?

Well, it turns out that birth order is actually a thing. More specifically, the more older brothers you have, if you're a boy, you have a higher chance of being gay. In the (much more reasonably named) journal *Hormones and Behavior,* Ray Blanchard of the University of Toronto concluded, "In men, sexual orientation correlates with an individual's number of older brothers, each additional older brother increasing the odds of homosexuality by approximately 33%."[14] Remember that guy's name; he comes up again later.

Unlike the Hamer study, this older brother thing has been reproduced many times and always with the same result. In 2020 the (very white sounding) *Proceedings of the Royal Society B* published that "In cross-analyzing data from 10 scientific studies with more than 5,000 subjects, researchers found that men with older brothers were 38 percent more likely to identify as gay."[15] If you're a gay man and you want to get with a Hemsworth brother, statistically speaking, you should hold out for Liam.

What does this have to do with being an only child?

I'm not a scientist, but "having older brothers" sure seems like the opposite of being an only child. OK, so having older brothers increases your chances of being gay. But why? Older sisters don't have the same effect on boys; we've studied that. Girls with older brothers also don't seem to be affected as far as we can tell. So what does having older brothers have to do with anything about a dude's sexuality? Turns out, it probably has less to do with the mere fact you have older brothers and more to do with the mother that carried you.

The "maternal immune hypothesis," also introduced by Ray Blanchard back in the mid-90s, may be the cause. Basically, because people that can give birth have two X chromosomes, the Y chromosome of a male presenting fetus looks foreign and bad to the immune system. Having a male fetus really irritates the XX person's plumbing, so to speak. This irritation results in the body fighting off the invader in the form of antibodies, and with practice, the body learns to do so more efficiently.

So, having multiple pregnancies with a Y chromosome involved will result in "anti-H-Y antibodies produced by the mother pass[ing] through the placental barrier to the fetus and affect[ing] aspects of sexual differentiation in the fetal brain." The irritation of the Y chromosome is like a grain of sand in an oyster, and each time the body gets better and better at turning it into a pearl. I very much like the idea of being gay as being a beautiful pearl, but now I'm very disturbed that I've compared a uterus to an oyster.

We've been led to believe by popular science that our genes are all that there is. In a world that believes that and has at times been obsessed with the idea that there is a "gay gene," this birth order thing is quite the conundrum. We've been taught to think that sexual reproduction is like a deck of cards where 50% of the cards come from our mother and 50% of the cards come from our father. Nature shuffles the cards and deals us the proverbial hand that we are dealt, and that's it. Done deal. But an incomplete understanding of biology has led many of us to believe that it is *our* hand, totally independent of everyone else's, including our siblings (unless we're identical births). This older brother thing shows us that just isn't true. It also shows us that the stereotype about only children is also untrue.

Kyle: *I'm going to ask them [Mike's brothers], "Did you know Mike is gay?" It's gonna be like a 5-minute conversation.*

Mike: *Do you have any other yes or no questions you want to ask them?*

EPISODE 004: BROTHERS (W/ MARTY AND MURPH JOHNSON)

Our genes interact with our environments. Before we're born, they interact with the womb that carries us. As we grow up, they interact with the things we put into our bodies, like food, water, and the air we breathe. Looking at our genome isn't a fully written play that just gets read out as we live our life. It's more like an improv show, where the cast interacts with the audience and with each other and makes something unexpected. And, like watching improv, life is better if you're drinking.

The fact our genes are only part of the story and are influenced by our environment and other factors like natural development is called epigenetics. The list of things that can be influenced by epigenetics is pretty wild. Things as varied as height, depression, addiction, and how fast your wounds heal all have potential epigenetic components.

I guess it's important to realize that "Born This Way" isn't just your genes. A lot of things about you were part of you at birth, or developed later through no fault of your own. A lot of things, sexuality included, certainly aren't about choice. All of these influences, whether genetic, epigenetic, or purely cultural, are all *tendencies* and not hard and fast rules.

This is not to be confused with the colloquial "nurture" we hear about in the so-called nature versus nurture debate. Most people think of nurture to be emotional, psychological, and cultural influences, especially from close family. The nurture crowd gives rise to parents blaming themselves for their child's sexuality. Epigenetics isn't that. There's nothing you did or didn't do, parents, that made Timmy want to bang Tommy instead of Tammy.

Having older brothers means you're more likely to be gay if you're a dude, but that's still a matter of chance. Imagine a bag of 100 marbles. Most of them are plain white boring marbles, but 25 of them are rainbow colored. Someone else's bag might have 75 of them rainbow colored. But you only get to pull one marble out of the bag, and you could easily pull a plain old boring marble out of either one. I have two younger brothers. That means my middle brother was born with more rainbow marbles in his bag, and my youngest brother with more rainbow marbles than both of us. But in the end, I'm the only one that's gay. I didn't choose to be gay; I just got lucky. And if I have any luck left to spend, universe, have Liam call me.

So, is the stereotype true?

The connection between being an only child and being a homosexual is rooted in antiquated ideas about the role of women and reproduction in society. None of the supposed negative outcomes of being an only child are supported by evidence, and, in fact, being an only child might be beneficial. *Not* being an only child, on the other hand, and specifically having older brothers if you're a boy, increases the chances you're gay.

What's the final verdict?

False.

SCORING YOUR QUIZ: QUESTION #2

In the quiz (page 40), we asked how many older brothers you have. Here's how to score your results:

a. 0: 0 gay points (despite the stereotype)
b. 1: 1 gay point
c. 2: 2 gay points
d. 3+: 3 gay points (you see where this is going...)

3

You Probably Have a Piercing in Your Right Ear

What's the stereotype?

The right ear is the gay ear to have pierced.

Is there really a gay ear?

Yup. When it comes to a single ear piercing, there's a common belief that one ear, the right ear, represents the gay ear. Anyone who has this ear pierced is signaling their gayness. (The left ear, mind you, is the straight ear.) When getting an ear piercing, many people have to look up online or ask their piercer which ear is the gay ear to be sure they don't send out a message they didn't mean to. Some gay people intentionally get their right ear pierced as a way to embrace their gayness and show it off to the world.

OK, Kyle, surely you're gay enough to have your ear pierced?

Nope, that's Mike. I don't have any piercings (or tattoos) at all. But I was interested in researching where this one came from. "The debate on whether there is a so-called gay ear is long over," proclaims a 2019 article in the *New York Times* about the modern trend of "single dangly earrings."[16] While it's interesting to see this once-reputable newspaper declaring the debate is over like a troll on Twitter who knows he lost, I'm not sure society is there yet. Many people grew up with the phrase "left is right, right is wrong," which indicated that the right ear was the gay ear, making it the wrong ear to pierce. Right = gay = wrong. That's why, Mike tells me, he only pierced his left because, at the time, he was in the closet.

In a way, this stereotype is more cut-and-dry than most. I hope no one reading this needs scientific confirmation that piercing your right ear doesn't turn you gay. (I would say right-wing politicians might need that spelled out for them, but I don't think they actually read the LBGTQ+ books they ban, so we're safe there.) Science may not know exactly what makes us gay (see Chapter 2), but it has nothing to do with our holes. Er, it has nothing to do with piercings. Society has ascribed meaning to something that, inherently, has none. That doesn't make it meaningless. Meaning derived from bullshit is still meaning.

Modern-day Westerners probably still associate earrings with femininity, in spite of growing acceptance among men. A 2007 study[17] of 400 US college students found that nearly 70% of women had any piercings vs. 28% of men, and men "were more likely to report that their parents/current and future friends would not approve of piercing." However, earrings have sometimes been seen as a sign of masculinity, for example, in 16th century Europe. These contradictory meanings are clear indications that there is no inherent femininity (or masculinity) to ear piercing. Socially constructed meanings catch on and spread through society by way of trendsetters or whispers or news articles. Throughout history, earrings have also been associated with holiness and sacrilege, nobility and barbarism, childhood and adulthood. Here are just a few examples I came across showing how various societies and religions have viewed earrings:

- The sacred Hindu tradition of Karnavedha calls for young children to have their ears pierced. Ancient Indian physician Sushruta said this provided "protection and decoration."[18]
- In 16th century Europe, men were more likely than women to wear earrings, as pointed out by the Puritanical Philip Stubbes in the 1583 *The Anatomy of Abuses* after calling people that wear them "dissolute minions."
- In 1900s America, earrings declined in popularity among women, partially as a negative reaction to European immigrants, who mostly all wore earrings. According to *The Berg Companion to Fashion*, critics called ear piercings "barbaric" and women who wore them "not quite respectable."[19]
- The *Encyclopedia of Body Adornment* says sailors pierced their ears to signal achievements like sailing around the world.[20] (I tried to confirm this one by watching the music video for *In the Navy,* but I was too distracted by the rhythm that overtook my body.)
- In a 1989 *Ebony* article (whose sub header read, "more and more men sport ornament once considered exclusively feminine"), *Miami Vice* actor Philip Michael Thomas explains that he pierced his left ear because, at a young age, a marine told him "that, in many places, particularly Africa, the wearing of an earring was the symbol of kings and royalty."[21]

So, when did the right one get gay?

It seems that the modern-day stereotype of the gay ear started in the 1960s as ear piercing was re-gaining popularity among women. By the late 1960s, men were following suit "thanks to the influence of the gay community and the hippies," as the *Encyclopedia of Body Adornment* put it. So, from its inception, the stereotype has been convoluted in that, even among men, it wasn't exclusively gay. Thanks, hippies. On the other hand, *Running the Gauntlet—An Intimate History of the Modern Body Piercing Industry* says that, in the 70s, "any white male who dared have his ear pierced might just as well have had the word 'GAY' tattooed on his forehead."[22] It may not have been exclusively gay, but perhaps it was still pretty gay.

Or perhaps each individual's take on what piercings mean depends heavily on their personal life experiences. In Hal Fischer's *Gay Semiotics,* a 1977 photograph-based project that documented gay men in the Castro, he showed how this community would signify their sexual interests using not only earrings, but also bandanas (using "the hanky code") and even keys hung from a metal clasp attached to a belt loop. Because of the criminalization and mistreatment of gay people, the use of subtle signals was common so that we could identify each other without giving ourselves away to the straights. Earrings were a cue, but a subtle one, which is a far cry from "GAY" tattooed on the forehead. As Fischer explained:

> An earring in the right lobe may suggest that the wearer prefers to play the passive role during sexual activity. Conversely, an earring in the left lobe may signify active behavior on the part of the wearer. Unlike the other signifiers, however, Right/Left placement of the earring is not always indicative of Passive/Active tendencies on the part of the wearer. Furthermore, the earring or stud is often adopted by non-homosexual men, thus making the earring the most subtle of homosexual signifiers.[23]

Given how strongly held our belief that there is, in fact, a "gay ear," it's surprising to see another example of how earrings were not considered exclusively gay. Instead, they were "subtle... signifiers." Even when they were being worn by gay men, at least in Fischer's experience, there wasn't one particular gay ear; both were gay in their own way. In other visual cues, like the hanky code, left and right placement was particularly important, with left indicating top (or "active") and right indicating bottom (or "passive"). However, with earrings, left and right placement were not as strongly correlated with top and bottom. Compare that to our modern saying that "right is wrong" where there's a clear importance to left vs. right. This additional layer of social construct was added somewhere along the way.

In 1984, a question appeared in Ann Landers' popular advice column asking about the meaning of a single earring and the left vs. right distinction. She answered that both straight and gay men might wear one, and that, for straight men, the different ears have no distinct meaning. On the other hand, among gays, she was told that the left ear "signifies the wish to be the dominant party" and the right "is making it known he prefers to play the submissive role." Her response echoed the information of *Gay Semiotics,* but her column came with a bit more mass (read: straight) appeal.

Nearly three months later, her column printed the responses she had received from readers. One straight man wrote that her answer was "just plain garbage" and that the earring in his left ear didn't

Mike: *My dad used to say, well before he knew that I was gay, "left is right, right is wrong."*

Kyle: *I never heard that growing up, but I found that when I was looking up information on this. Another thing people used to say is "left ear buccaneer, right ear queer."*

Mike: *Buck an ear? That's how I buy corn!*

EPISODE 052: HANKY CODE

mean anything. (I'd argue this confirmed the answer she provided, but perhaps he was just angry at his incorrect assumption that he'd been compared to a gay.) Another response said a right ear piercing meant opposition to the Vietnam war. Thanks, hippies. Yet another said a right ear piercing means a man is divorced. A final letter, in addition to calling her "some kind of dummy," said that left meant Democrat and right meant Republican. (Suddenly, I kinda like the phrase "left is right and right is wrong.")

I saw the debate about the precise meaning of left and right ear piercings continue on even today. The comments section of a 2022 Queerty article on the topic contained similar disputes, such as one user who said, "Upon my growing up in eastern MA, in the 1960s and early 70s, the earring in the left ear was the signal for being a gay man."[24] No one seemed to be able to agree on exactly which ear piercing meant what. So where did the concept that "left is right and right is wrong" come from?

I can't pin it down precisely, but the closest I could find is a 1991 *New York Times* article about the "piercing fad," saying that gay men "often [wore] a single piece of jewelry in the right ear to indicate sexual preference."[25] The context of left as top and right as bottom had been lost. Then again, I'm not surprised that, somewhere along the way, the right ear became the gay ear. The journey of a gay stereotype often starts with femininity, then progresses to gay by way of the bottoms.

In a section of the article titled "A Gay Signal Is Lost," the *Times* laments that, "in the last few years, so many heterosexual men have begun wearing earrings [...] that the placement no longer suggests anything about sexual preference." An interesting take given the *Encyclopedia of Body Adornment, Gay Semiotics,* and Ann Landers had all pointed out that non-gay people wore earrings, so it was never an exclusively gay signal. By (misleadingly) pointing out that the right ear no longer meant gay, how much did they reinforce the idea into public consciousness? By commenting on its death, they might have given it life.

"If a girl has a pierced tongue, she'll probably suck your dick," Chris Rock said in his 1999 comedy track, "No Sex (in the Champagne Room)." I remember watching the video on MTV when I was in my early teens, realizing that tongue rings had a sexual connotation. The line continues, "If a guy has a pierced tongue, he'll probably suck your dick." I didn't understand exactly why I was aroused by that part. (There was truth to that line because, as it turns out, a guy with a pierced tongue did end up sucking my dick in college.) The more important truth is that piercings come with social meaning, and sometimes it's sexual.

Did young Kyle know about this gay ear thing?

While I don't remember hearing the phrase "left is right and right is wrong" growing up, I knew that there was a gay ear, and if you were going to pierce your ear, you should be extra careful not to accidentally get the wrong ear, i.e. the gay ear, pierced. I always got confused on which ear it was, one of my many sources of gay confusion over the course of my life. What wasn't confusing was the message I got from my classmates: avoid the gay ear because being gay is bad. The idea of a gay/bad ear was just one of the many microaggressions that chipped away at my feelings of self-worth.

I'm not the only one who has realized as an adult that I had some leftover issues from this specific microaggression. In 2016, researchers followed two LGBTQ+ student teachers. Over the course of the year-long case study, one of the participants, a gay male teacher, learned that students were calling him gay behind his back. His initial response to the first grader that informed him was, "that's not nice." He was later embarrassed by this gut reaction, but he was so used to the word "gay" being used as an insult. Gay is bad. Gay is negative. Even when we're publicly out and content with our gay-ness, we still have to work to unlearn these instinctual reactions we were taught growing up. He did, in fact, have an earring on the right ear.

"The debate on whether there is a so-called gay ear is long over." I keep thinking about that statement. Then, I think about all the ar-ticles I saw on the topic on sites like Queerty and Yahoo! Entertain-ment and PopSugar and The Cut and Mel Magazine and countless others. I saw Reddit posts and Quora questions and YouTube vid-eos. Everything I saw was posted between 2016–2023. Most sources come to a similar, rightful conclusion that gender stereotypes are becoming a thing of the past, and this one is outdated. As Queerty says in its article, "it doesn't matter which ear is the gay ear."

However, that feels like an idealistic future state we want to work towards. A lovely dream, not actual reality. Each of these articles also reminds its readers that the right ear is the one that has been known as the gay ear. This is the information people who came across the articles were presumably seeking. I think the fact that so many re-sources are still being written on the topic means it's still on our pub-lic consciousness. It can't be erased from our collective memory that easily. There seems to be some generational microaggression-based trauma we're still working through as adults. Not everyone remem-bers the stereotype that the right ear is the gay ear. For some of us, it was a different ear or it meant a different thing. But for those of us who did experience it, it still feels like left is right and right is wrong.

So, is the stereotype true?

This one is an odd stereotype to judge because it's completely built around the meaning society creates. Obviously ear piercings don't make anyone gay. What's true is that, at least in the modern US, so-ciety has decided that the right ear is the ear to pierce if you're gay.

This hasn't always been the case, and there seems to be some historical context that was lost along the way. In gay men, the right ear originally meant bottom and the left ear meant top, so technically, either ear could be the gay ear. However, homophobic phrases like "left is right and right is wrong" have solidified that, in today's world, we have all agreed that the right ear is, in fact, the gay ear.

What's the final verdict?

Mostly true.

SCORING YOUR QUIZ: QUESTION #3

In the quiz (page 14), we asked if your right ear is pierced. Here's how to score your results:

a. No: 0 gay points
b. Yes, and I know it's the gay ear: 2 gay points
c. Yes, and so is the left ear: 1 gay point

You Probably Have Limp Wrists

What's the stereotype?

Certain body movements, especially limp wrists, indicate a man is gay on sight alone.

I've seen this in so many movies and TV shows. What gives?

The "limp-wristed gay" is a stereotype that we've seen portrayed in media for a long time, from TV sketch comedy shows to movies. However, the idea that a limp wrist is feminine and therefore potentially indicative of homosexuality is much, much older than that. These cultural ideas may not have come out of the blue, though. Limp wrists, and body movements in general, may actually be part of our physiology and influenced by our sexuality.

Hey, Mike, do gay dudes really have limp wrists?

Lord knows I thought I did. My family, specifically my mom's family, is bananas. (Thank you Gwen Stefani for making it so I never misspell that word.) Our family reunions are truly a spectacle. We're fond of dressing up, wearing silly hats, making skits, and sometimes holding a parade (even if our host city hasn't invited us). It's bananas. I took Kyle once to Easter Saturday, and I think he's scarred for life.

In the late 80s and early 90s, camcorders really became ubiquitous. Suddenly, it seemed like grandparents everywhere had one and used it to record every detail of every family event, mine included. If you remember America's Funniest Home Videos, I'm pretty sure that show had a lot to do with everyone suddenly becoming a documentarian. As a result, there's hours and hours and hours of footage of shit on VCR tapes hiding in American closets that absolutely nobody should care about or ever be forced to see. One tape in particular, however, changed my life.

I'm guessing I was about 12, and I was right at the beginning of that horrific time of biological change known as puberty. It was then that at one of these ridiculous family reunions, we had a parade. I don't remember a theme to this one. I think it was 4th of July weekend and it was just a run-of-the-mill parade for America's birthday. I joined in the fun holding a small US flag, waving it around as we marched. Later in the year we went to my grandparents' house and as we often did, got out the tapes of past family reunions to remember the fun.

There I was, looking at myself on screen, and I was mortified. What I saw and felt disturbed me so much, I had to leave the room. I heard my internal monologue say, "look at the limp wrists on that faggot with the flag." Was that faggot with the flag really me? Could other people see what I was seeing on the screen? Did I always look that gay? I certainly couldn't ask these questions; I felt like I had nobody to talk to. It was the loneliest feeling in the world.

You see, it was around that time, 12 or 13 years old, that I was starting to realize that instead of having feelings about girls like my male friends, I was starting to have feelings for boys. Puberty is kind of a bitch for everyone, but for a gay boy in conservative Eastern

Washington in the 80s, it was terrifying. I knew being gay was dangerous and wrong, or so I thought at the time, so I did everything in my power to not be. In retrospect, I clearly went through all of the stages of grief over this crisis of sexuality. Denial and bargaining were the strongest stages and took the longest for me to get through before finally coming out at 30.

Anyway, that video of myself was a life-altering wake up call. I became intent on fixing my wrists before they betrayed my secrets. I would practice in a mirror, holding onto things with a manly grip. I worked hard to learn how to gesticulate with only strong and rigid wrist positions. I was practicing the skills I needed to reinforce with concrete the closet I'd decided to stay in at all costs. But where did I get the idea that limp wrists would out me as a gay person? It clearly was something I automatically saw and associated with homosexuality.

Could it have just been culture? There are plenty of examples to draw from.

I remember in particular a character on Saturday Night Live, played by Dana Carvey, named "Lyle the Effeminate Heterosexual."[26] In it, a lisping hairdresser named Lyle goes through different scenarios in which he finds out that because of his unforgivable flamboyance different people in his life believe he is gay. Even his wife, played by Jan Hooks, at one point confronts him about his orientation. It was a recurring sketch, complete with an opening jingle and a montage, reminiscent of a terrible sitcom. One of the that's-just-too-gay-for-him-to-be-straight images in that opening is, you guessed it, Lyle with full on cracked limp wrists. That sketch aired for the first time in 1989 when I had just turned 11 years old, and I already knew what it all meant. Lyle moved and spoke effeminately, and that meant he was gay and less of a man.

Lyle on SNL is not the first example of movement and speech being tied to masculinity and sexual orientation. One of the earliest examples of exploring this theme in cinema is the 1956 film Tea and Sympathy, an adaptation of a 1953 stage play of the same name. In both versions, a college freshman named Tom Lee is chastised by his classmates for not being masculine enough. In the stage version, he was explicitly accused of being homosexual. But for the film version, in 1950s Hollywood and under the Hays Code, you couldn't make a potentially gay character into someone the audience would feel sympathy for. In fact, in 1956, Bob Thomas of the Associated Press wrote that "many said it could never be made into a movie."[27]

To get around this, the studio removed all explicit references to Tom being homosexual, and neither that word nor any other referring to queer sexuality appears in the film. Instead, they attach every gay stereotype they could think of to the character of Tom, to make it very clear without ever actually saying it that any reasonable person would immediately realize Tom knows what penises taste like.

In the first 15 minutes of the movie, he:

- plays guitar and sings a song about "the grief of love"
- stares wistfully out the window
- demonstrates he knows a lot about flowers and which ones to plant to add a bit of blue to the garden (forget-me-nots, by the way)
- says his father disapproved of his hobbies
- talks about having an absentee father who "wasn't around much"
- discloses he is a child of divorce
- shows strong evidence of being a mama's boy when interacting with his teacher's wife, Mrs. Reynolds
- says he plays tennis but isn't hanging out with his teammates

- reveals he's in the drama club
- ...and actively rehearsing as an actor for the school play
- ...and has been cast as a female role
- ...and Mrs. Reynolds is making a beautiful dress for him
- says he's never been in love, and implies he's never had sex
- explains he's on the dance committee
- asks Mrs. Reynolds what color her dress is so he can pick out a corsage
- says he doesn't know any girls, even back home, because he only went to all-boys boarding schools (hot, right?)
- says he'd rather talk with girls than dance
- reads *Candida* under a shady tree for his "outdoor time"
- admits to being kind of a creeper and spying on people when they swim
- criticizes one woman's sewing technique, and then takes over for her
- talks about growing up with a maid in a way that makes him seem soft
- says he's a good cook, to which one of the women says "someday you'll make some girl a good wife"
- has to be forced to play catch with the other boys, who then reject him
- seems reluctant to join in on the shirtless beach wrestling
- gets called "Sister Boy" by his classmates
- moves around in a slightly femme, graceful way, including limp wrists.

He also misses out on the quiz the boys are taking. They have a magazine they're passing around on the beach and in it is a quiz called "are you masculine?" With such scintillating questions as "which of these is most fun: reading, hunting, or gardening?" The answer with the most masculine points, by the way, was hunting. But a quiz that tells you how masculine you are? What a ridiculous idea, right? Who would publish that?

Anyway, the limp-wristed stereotype often gets intertwined with other body movements, especially putting your hands on your hips. While closed fists against your hips makes you look like a warrior, if your hands are unclenched it's difficult to put them on your hips without bending your wrists one way or the other. Either way you bend those wrists, hands on hips makes you look gay. Tom's wrists are already a little bendy, if you know what I mean, but in a heart to heart with his roommate Al, he puts his hands on his hips. The gay way, with bent wrists. Al, the paragon of straight boy masculinity, tries to help Tom butch up his body language.

For all the coding they do to Tom's character without ever using the words gay or homosexual, it all only works because those ideas were already firmly present in the culture. They don't have to say Tom is gay; we can see it.

This limp wrists thing must go back even further, then.

Indeed. In 1919, almost 40 years before Tea and Sympathy, there was a trial of someone accused of homosexuality in Rhode Island. At one point the judge asked a witness how gay men identified each other. The witness said a gay man "acted sort of peculiar, walking around with his hands on his hips... the expression with the eyes and the gestures."[28] Hands on hips again, and we know what that means. (Hint: gay limp wrists.)

In George Chauncey's excellent book *Gay New York*,[29] he points out that "how to spot a gay" based on appearances was already common knowledge in the 1870s. In that book, he includes a reproduction of a pamphlet distributed to Latin American businessmen to show them the different kinds of characters on the streets of New York. In addition to sex workers and beggars, it includes "fairies," complete with pictures of a typical one of each. In the illustration of the fairy, the homosexual in question has possibly the limpest wrist on a cartoon I've ever seen.

How far back do we have to go?

When looking at limp wrists, some people point to the 17th and 18th centuries. High fashion during this period had women's dresses that were sometimes so tight they couldn't really bend their elbows or shoulders, so they would gesture with only their wrists. As we've said, the stereotype of femininity at some point gets attributed to the gays.

But this limp wrists thing goes back even further, to at least the Romans. They thought a limp wrist meant you were less of a man. They didn't think it meant you were gay, which would be ironic coming from them if they did since they would bang each other in the butt all the time. But it definitely meant there was something wrong with you if you were a dude. Some Roman orators, which I just learned is not the name for someone who bottoms with their mouth, including Quintilion and possibly Cicero, advised strongly against moving your hands, including wrist position, in a way that would detract from your speeches by making you appear less masculine.[30]

Cultural ideas about gender come and go, even to the degree that pink used to be for boys and blue used to be for girls. So, if this idea about wrists pops up over and over again throughout history and through different kinds of media, maybe there's actually something to it that is making it stick? Science nerds have taken a look at it.

One study looking at body types and motion had volunteers walk on a treadmill for two minutes. Cameras would capture their motion and process it into 3D animations. Think something like the deeply creepy Tom Hanks in the deeply creepy Polar Express. For the first part of the study, the science nerds were specifically looking at "shoulder swagger and hip sway" when different people walked.[31]

They found that gay subjects, men and women, had more "gender-incongruent" body types and movements. The gay men had more of an hourglass shape and swayed their hips more than their straight counterparts. Lesbians had more "tubular" bodies and more swagger in their shoulders than straight girls. Now say the word tubular like a surfer dude, because you really have to after that.

But that was just the data about body shapes. For the second part of the study, those scientists wanted to find out if people can see gayness in videos of other humans. Was there something about the way people move on camera, things like wrists and hips, that let us reliably detect sexuality?

Observers were shown the videos from the first part of the study of the subjects on the treadmill, but only from the back so they couldn't see their faces. After watching two minutes of treadmill walking, the volunteers were able to correctly identify the sexual orientation of the subject "significantly better than chance"... but only when they were dudes. Turns out the observers in the experiment weren't great at picking out the lesbians, but were pretty good at seeing a little swishiness when it came to the gay men.

Mike: *(Christians) have magical thinking. If your son being gay gives him a limp wrist, breaking his wrist is not going to make him straight. The limp wrist is not magic. It's not making the dicks go into his mouth.*

Kyle: *Someone Tweeted "my dad suspected I was gay so he made me go chop down trees to make me more of a man. Joke's on you, Dad, now I suck dicks and can chop wood."*

EPISODE 215: LIMP WRISTS

Does that mean gay men are swishy by biology, and they can't even help themselves?

Well, it's a little dangerous to say that biological sex and cultural attitudes about gender are in lockstep with each other. Human sexuality and gender expression are incredibly complicated and I'm not qualified to pick it all apart. But it does seem like there are certain things, like body proportions and, yes, the way we move our bodies including our wrists, that are at least influenced by our sexual orientation, and our fellow humans can see it.

Young Mike could see it in himself, and he was right. I wish I didn't feel like I had to practice in the mirror to "fix" my body language. I wish I could go back in time and give myself a hug and say "those limp wrists on that faggot with the flag in that video are nothing to be ashamed of." If I could, I might have saved myself a lot of years.

So, is the stereotype true?

Like a lot of things, this one isn't a slam dunk. You can only count on body movements like a person's wrists to get you a guess that is "significantly better than chance," but that still leaves a wide margin for error. And it only works with gay dudes, apparently, which is pretty wild. Given the inconsistencies between genders and the fact that "better than chance" isn't a very high bar, it's hard to say the science is conclusive. But cultural ideas about these things have persisted, over millennia, in a way that seems hard to completely dismiss.

What's the final verdict?

Mostly true.

SCORING YOUR QUIZ: QUESTION #4

In the quiz (page 14), we asked if anyone has ever described your movements as "swishy." Here's how to score your results:

a. Yes, and I fixed that shit: 2 gay points (because repression is real, y'all)

b. Yes, and this is who I am, goddammit: 2 gay points (own that swish!)

c. No, why would they?: 0 gay points

d. No, my feet don't move when I dance: -1 gay point

5

You're Probably Hot and Jacked

What's the stereotype?

Gay men are all hot and jacked.

What's the harm in that?

Gay men are stereotypically viewed as hotter than straight men. It's seen as a compliment to gay men. They're expected to care more about their bodies and appearance, which places additional burdens on their everyday life. They're supposed to go to the gym, to moisturize, to always be well put-together. Straight men, on the other hand, are schlubby. The entire premise of *Queer Eye for the Straight Guy* is that we're like magical gay elves that can fix your appearance in a weekend. Gay men are hot, according to the stereotype.

Kyle, you've talked about having body issues before, yeah?

It was in elementary school when I first told my mom I thought I was fat. I don't remember where I got the idea, or even what my mom said in response. I just remember feeling like I was fat. That feeling has been with me ever since.

I was always a tall kid. I'm 6'3" now, and most of my life has been spent explaining to people that yes, I played basketball growing up, but I don't anymore because, in spite of my height, I'm actually really bad at it. I always wished I was a little shorter so I didn't get tall comments or stand out so much. I hated being called "big man" by my basketball coaches.

I think I was always an average weight, too, but it's hard for me to be objective. Never in my life have I felt comfortable with the way my body looked. Maybe I felt OK about myself one year in college where I almost had abs, but that's the best I can remember.

What I also remember about college is that, as part of my new-found freedom, I could eat whatever I wanted. I would often buy vanilla icing and eat most of it right from the can with a spoon. Whenever I did that, I would then spend the next two weeks running every single day to try to burn off the embarrassment. (It wasn't until I was an adult that I'd learn the term "binge eating.")

I've tried to care about exercise, but it's never quite stuck for me. For someone who has such a negative view of their own body, I never managed to do something about it. After I eat a whole pizza or a whole container of Oreos, I try to diet or do some exercise to work it off, but I've never developed a routine. I'm stuck in this perpetual state of hating how I look and not being able to bring myself to fix it. Then again, I don't think it would matter if I could change my body overnight into a porn star body. No matter what I've looked like, I've always hated my body. I think a part of me always will.

It got worse after I came out in college. The expectations of gay men are that they wear clothes that become the trend (I prefer an old t-shirt and jeans), that they're well-manicured head to toe (I don't know a thing about skin care routines or hairstyles), that they're hot (I don't know, I think I'm OK looking), and that they're buff (I can confirm I'm definitely not buff). Gay men hang out at the gym enough that the community has sexualized it, sometimes calling it "gay church." I'm afraid of it because it reminds me of how I'll never fit in with the fit crowd.

Some people, usually straight women, have lamented to me that gay men are all so much hotter than straight men. There was even a study[32] that quantified this effect. Researchers showed non-homophobic college-aged straight women pictures of men. When the women believed the men were gay, they judged them as "significantly more physically attractive" than when they thought the men were straight. (The same effect doesn't happen when straight men rated lesbians.) The study referred to this phenomenon as the "gay-pretty-boy stereotype," and while I'm surprised someone took the time to quantify it, I'm not surprised it's real.

At the gay clubs, there's often a go-go boy with a hot body and amazing dance moves getting tips. It's always a reminder of who I'll never be. At Pride, there are jacked boys in their underwear, dancing on floats, waving at the crowd as they show off their hot bodies. It's another reminder of who I'll never be. The guys on gay porn have huge dicks and hot bodies, the epitome of gay desire. Yet another reminder of who I'll never be. The gay characters on TV shows and gay influencers on Instagram and guys that reject me on Grindr. There are a million different places that I can find a reminder that gay guys are supposed to be hot, muscled, sexy studs.

Seeing constant reminders that gay men are supposed to be hot can hurt. It can take me down a spiral in my head. If gay men are supposed to be so hot, what's wrong with me? Why aren't I one of those hot gay men? Maybe I don't work on myself enough, and maybe I could never be the person that they expect me to be. Maybe I'll never be happy with how I look, and I'm just the lone gay who feels like an unattractive blob.

Gross. Why do we feel like this?

In an interview with Good Morning America,[33] a man named Nicko Cassidy said, "I think it's definitely deep rooted the shame from childhood and growing up just to be who we are." I grew up wishing I was someone entirely different (i.e. straight) and feeling shame about who I was at my very core. It would make sense, then, that I'd grow up to feel ashamed of all of me, including my physical body. If I hate myself, I hate *all* of myself.

Mike: *I was at the Renaissance Festival in Kansas City yesterday, and I gave my ID to this lady from whom I wanted to purchase Dragon's Breath, a cocktail. Anyway, she said, "you, sir, are aging very well," and I had mixed feelings about that.*

EPISODE 140: BRITNEY SPEARS

It's a wonder that it was at such a young age that I first expressed my disappointment in my own body. I don't even remember liking a boy until junior high. (*Oh, Daniel.*) So, what was it that I was responding to? Maybe a part of me knew to hate myself before I even came to understand who I was. Maybe I internalized homophobia before I even realized that I was a homo.

Body dysmorphia is the excessive fixation in perceived flaws in appearance, and I think that's what we're talking about here. Most definitions I saw included the fact that the perceived flaws are usually minor or can't be seen by other people. I don't know if what I have meets the bar for a medical diagnosis, but I can relate to some of the symptoms, such as being extremely preoccupied with the perceived flaw (for me, my weight and my stomach), constantly comparing myself to others, and having perfectionist tendencies.

My body image issues have even affected my relationships. In my first long-term relationship, I told my then boyfriend that he wasn't allowed to touch my stomach. I felt so self-conscious about it, just having another person put their hand there made me want to curl up in a ball and hide. It was like a spotlight shining on one of my biggest insecurities. While he respected my wishes, he also expressed his disappointment. He told me he loved me and my body and wanted to be able to touch it. I didn't realize until that moment that my body image could affect areas of my life outside of my own self-esteem. I eventually came around and let him touch my stomach, even though I never came around to believe that anyone would actually prefer my specific body type.

Beyond relationships, body image issues affect our sex lives, too. After my second major relationship, I was at my heaviest at 270 pounds. (This isn't a number I thought I'd share with anyone, ever.) I found myself, once again, back on the hookup apps. While I don't remember seeing "no fats, no fems" explicitly written on a profile, I felt like I was being haunted by the idea. I had a hard time, and not in a good way. It seemed like no one was interested in me.

One study found that 42% of gay men reported that "their feelings about their body had negative effects on the quality of their sex life," compared to only 22% of straight men.[34] I dieted and lost a good amount of weight, and I felt better about myself. It seemed like it made a difference; I got more responses on the apps and hooked up more. Was it because my physical appearance had changed, or because I felt more comfortable in my body? I can't possibly know for sure. But there's part of me that believes my weight made it harder for me to find sex in the gay world.

I know I'm not the only one that feels that physical appearance is extremely important in the community, based solely on the conversations I have with my friends and with listeners of the podcast. But researchers have confirmed it, too. One study[35] measuring body image concerns of gay men, straight men, and straight women noted that "gay men (like women) believed their physical appearance was more important to others than did heterosexual men." They also found that the more important we believed physical characteristics were *to other people,* the lower our self-esteem. In my case, the more I think everyone cares about my weight, the worse I feel about myself. The paper states that this "perhaps reflect[s] increased pressure within the gay community to attain the ideal body shape." I wonder if, the more we comment on gay men's obsession with appearance, the more pressure we feel about our own appearance, which lowers our self-esteem. I wonder if, simply by writing this, I'm contributing to the very issue I'm struggling with.

In trying to determine if our body image issues result in any measurable differences in our actual bodies, I came across a 2010 NBC News article[36] titled, "Gay guys really are thinner, study says." In it, the author mentions that researchers found that 14% of gay men were obese (vs. 21% of straight men). It turns out, the opposite was true of women: straight women were less likely to be obese than lesbians. The title of that article seems misleading to me. With the research's findings, the most I would say is that gay men are less likely to be obese, which is very different than being thin. It may seem like a linguistic technicality, but I think so many people are looking for proof of what they already believe—that gay men are supposed to be hotter and thinner—that it brings bias into whatever they're doing, be it writing a headline or doing research.

I also think there's a tangible impact to sensationalized articles like the NBC News one. Skimming a headline that says that gays are thinner validates the fears that I already have, that I'm supposed to be thinner than my straight friends. Queerty's article[37] reporting on the same study was called "Why Are Gay Men Thinner Than Hetero Guys (And Lesbians Fatter Than Straight Girls)?" I know they need their clicks, but discussion of gay men's issues with their body, and the gay community's obsession with body image, are everywhere. We're obsessed with being obsessed with our bodies.

Maybe it's fair, though. If gay men are way more body image conscious than straight men, it merits discussion. Some research makes this claim directly. The study I mentioned earlier, the one about gay men's body image and their sex life, states that "existing research provides reasonable evidence that more gay men than heterosexual men report dissatisfaction with their bodies." Other studies have a slightly different take. A meta-review of 27 different studies concluded that there's only "a small, but real, difference between heterosexual and gay men in terms of body satisfaction." I guess the research isn't as sold that we have a huge body image issue.

Wait, you're saying maybe it's not just the gay guys?

A paper called "Revisiting Gay Men's Body Image Issues: Exposing the Fault Lines" explores why previous studies may have overstated the gay community's obsession with body image. They talk about very research-y things, like methodology and data analysis. They conclude that gay men's body image issues are more "announced rather than pronounced," meaning they're discussed far more than is merited. In what I can only read as an academic slap to the face, they state that "future researchers and theorists are invited to resist evaluations that reduce gay men to being universally fixated on their appearance."[38]

If, in reality, gay men are only slightly more concerned about their body image than straight men, why is this such a major topic of conversation within the gay community? Perhaps AIDS had an impact on the way we viewed our bodies and the importance of being fit. Perhaps the media, magazines, and porn we consume puts hot bodies on a pedestal. Perhaps our myriad of classifications for gay men based on their bodies—twinks, bears, daddies, etc.—makes us particularly focused on appearance. Perhaps the fact that we are attracted to our own gender makes us more likely to compare our bodies to others. In reality, all of these likely contribute to the discourse in their own way. However, I think the very assumption that gay men are hotter than straight men is part of the issue.

This idea is being discussed, not just within gay communities, but within society as a whole. On TheStudentRoom.co.uk, a random website I found when researching this topic, someone posted the question "Why Are Gay guys hotter than Straight guys?! (no homo)." One person replied that most male models are gay. Someone else said that gay men know what they find attractive in a man, so they know how to make themselves attractive. Many others said that gay men have a better sense of fashion. I gathered a few things from the post: (1) people expect gay men to be hotter than straight men, (2) people use gay stereotypes regularly when trying to answer the question of "why," and (3) there are lots of insecure straight guys that include "no homo" in their answer to make extra sure everyone knows that, even though they're talking about gay men's attractiveness, they're not gay.

What if gay men are just somehow objectively more attractive?

I tried to find out the actual truth behind the differences in the bodies of gay and straight men. It's already a hard question to answer, and it's even harder to do without reinforcing fatphobia, conventional standards of beauty, and gay stereotypes. We do know that gay men tend to *want* a more muscular, leaner body than straight men.[39] Unfortunately, there are no studies that conclusively confirm or deny whether gay men are more attractive than straight men. So, I'll just mention some of the physical differences research has found, and you can draw your own conclusions about whether you think that's more or less attractive:

- As previously mentioned, research shows gay men are less likely to be overweight than straight men.
- Surprisingly, gay men are more likely to be shorter than straight men and have smaller limbs compared to their body's trunk.[40] (Given how tall I am, I'm proof that averages don't apply to individuals.)
- Straight men's faces were measured and found to be more symmetrical than gay men's.[41]
- While some studies simply state that gay men's faces appear more feminine than straight men's, one study added more depth to the conversation by examining specifics. They found that gay men "showed relatively wider and shorter faces, smaller and shorter noses, and rather massive and more rounded jaws, resulting in a mosaic of both feminine and masculine features."[42]
- One study found that gay men have bigger penises than straight men. In fact, the study states they were "significantly larger penises (in both length and circumference)." Be still, my beating hole.

Taller men with symmetrical faces are typically revered as attractive in our society, so those points would go to the straight men. However, thinner and bigger penises would give points to gay men. So, really, there can't (and won't) be a definitive answer as to whether gay men really are hotter than straight men. Beyond that, people of all shapes, sizes, and penises can be attractive, so each person's preference on what they like in a man's appearance will play a role.

I wish I could internalize the idea that body types come in all shapes and sizes, and there are some people, including my ex-boyfriend, who like and appreciate the way I look. I'm not there yet. In fact, as I'm writing this, I'm dieting because it's Pride month, and that's the month that gays are supposed to be at their hottest.

As I'm working on my mental health in therapy, I'm also working on my appreciation for my own body. I can sometimes find myself trapped in a logical fallacy that says if I'm working on my physical appearance, like working out or exercising, that must mean I'm unhappy with how I look and I want it to change, meaning the way I am is bad. I'm trying to remember that I can both appreciate who I am and what I look like, today, while also setting goals for myself and striving to improve. I can do both at the same time, and the ideas don't have to be in conflict. With more work, I hope I can eventually grow out of the little boy who once told his mom he thought he was fat.

Mike: *A bear is a big, hairy, burly gay guy.*

Kyle: *Something I liked in the Urban Dictionary definition was "a cuddly body," which is the nice way of saying "fat."*

Ma Johnson: *Or just short for your weight.*

EPISODE 007: MOTHER
(W/ PATTY JOHNSON)

So, is the stereotype true?

Are gay men hotter than straight men? Surprisingly, researchers *have* found measurable physical differences between gay and straight men. Gay men are less likely to be obese, more likely to be shorter, less likely to have a symmetrical face, and more likely to have a bigger penis. I don't think any of that gives us enough clear evidence to declare one group the winner. What we do know is that stereotypes about gay men's bodies are rampant, though our body image issues (compared to straight men) are largely overstated. There isn't any evidence that says that gay men are hotter than straight men, other than unfounded assumptions about what a gay man is "supposed" to look like.

What's the final verdict?

False.

SCORING YOUR QUIZ: QUESTION #5

In the quiz (page 14), we asked how you would describe your torso. Here's how to score your results:

- **a.** 6 pack: o gay points
- **b.** 8 pack: o gay points
- **c.** Half rack: o gay points

(If you have abs, good for you, but you don't get any points for it here. Gay men aren't inherently hotter or more jacked than straight men. Not all gays have abs.)

6

You Probably Had a 4.0 GPA

What's the stereotype?

Gays are overachievers, especially academically.

Gays put the anal in anal retentive

He struts into a room with a rainbow of highlighters in one hand and a stack of perfectly organized flashcards in the other. His GPA? As flawless as his hair, it's a 4.0. His planner has more color-coding than a unicorn's dream journal, and he's definitely going to ruin the curve for everyone else on this next exam. Is this boy gay?

Hey Mike, is this like the "gay wedding coordinator with a clipboard" or something?

Close, but not exactly. There's certainly some overlap there. A gay best friend yelling at bridesmaids is also a stereotype rooted in a relentless pursuit of perfection. But here, we're talking about a focus on self-achievement, especially in academics.

The concept of the overachieving gay is simple: gay people, boys especially, because of powerful cultural messaging, internalize the idea that their queerness is bad. So, they become the "best little boy in the world" (yes, the theory is actually called that) in order to compensate for that perceived flaw. The best little boy in the world is perfect and perfectly worthy of love, and becoming him is the perfect way to compensate for the ugliness of being queer. There is something about the theory that seems plausible, right? Our culture instills ideas about masculinity, heterosexuality, achievement, and the need to prove ourselves.

Of all the ways we teach children to evaluate their worth relative to the other children, grade point average is probably the earliest. It's also one of the few places in life where there is an achievable perfection, an objective upper limit, which in the US anyway is usually a 4.0. There are places where higher than a 4.0 is possible. If there's one thing parents are fucking crazy about it's their fucking children, and some places have a "better than perfect." I'm not touching any of that psychopathy with a 10 foot pole here; let's just pretend 4.0 is perfection.

In a universe where a kid believes at their core they are flawed for any reason, but especially because they are gay, what better way to compensate than numeric perfection? Now it seems a little silly that you might think a 4.0 GPA will make a bigoted world love you despite the sodomy, but these kinds of psychological symbolic tradeoffs rarely make sense. They're also not conscious a lot of the time.

Did you know any of these hyper-performing gays growing up?

I had a friend, a year younger than me in school, and I'll just call him J. J and I met in 1983. His older brother and I were classmates, and our families lived on the same street. Street is a strong word; it was a rural road with a 50 mph speed limit. But the three of us (him, myself, and his older brother) were all close enough in age that we quickly became a pack. My first interaction with J was talking about Transformers, very much a part of every boy's active vocabulary in the early 80s. Kids at that stage have no sexuality, and none of us knew that two out of the three of us would grow up to be into dudes.

J was always so creative and hilarious. I remember talking about Star Wars, designing the next epic Lego structure we'd build, and drawing pictures on the exposed drywall of their basement. He was a chubby kid, so in early adolescence when he became rail thin, I'm sad we praised his transformation instead of recognizing it for the dysfunction it probably was. A different kind of cry for attention than grades, perhaps.

As we got older, we reached the age where sexuality started to develop. Although both of us handled our secrets by heading into the closet, J and I had very different experiences. There are some queer kids, like myself for the most part, who have the privilege of "passing" as straight as we grow up. That is to say, our mannerisms, patterns of speech, and ability to conform to societal expectations lets us fly under the radar. That might have been because I was practicing (see Chapter 4). J was not one of those kids. The movie Mean Girls has the line "too gay to function," and that was J. You could just hear it in his voice. You could see it in his eccentricities.

In high school, we were in drama together. Drama collects misfits. It also collects homosexuals (see Chapter 13). He was a good actor. Really good. I mean probably not by objective standards (high school theater is fucking terrible), but at least within our little world, he was tremendous. But if theater was the gayest thing about me, J had a much harder time keeping his fabulousness under control. Too gay to function.

Now, J wasn't out, but everyone sort of knew. And whether it was because the other boys assumed he was gay or for other reasons, J was certainly bullied for being different. I'm sure you saw this coming given the topic of the chapter: J was a 4.0 student. He was valedictorian of his class.

The whole time growing up, our families were quite close, and it seemed to me that the boy was driven by something other than just loving to study. It felt like he was compensating. When J finally came out, just before his high school graduation, the administration refused to let him give his valedictorian speech without edits they demanded. His speech talked about the rampant homophobia of our little shit ass town and the failure of the school to protect him. They didn't like that. Speaking truth to power can be dangerous. Just like white people hate being called racist more than they hate racism, straight people hate being called homophobic more than they hate homophobia. So the speech had to change. I'm trying to remember now what made the final edit, but one definite result: J was gay, officially, and everyone knew. His mom, who in a lot of ways was like a mother to me too, told him, "I love you, and accept you; please just don't get AIDS and die." So, now he was out, and his dramatic scholastic achievements suddenly seemed to make more sense.

So, is the 4.0 GPA gay really a thing?

In 1973 Andrew Tobias, under the pseudonym John Reid, authored a book called *The Best Little Boy in the World.*[43] Frankly, I think any gay worth his salt could have done a lot better than "John Reid" for a fake name, but that's just me being a bitch. The book chronicles his growing up closeted in a very different America than today's, and how he flagellated himself into being as perfect as possible to compensate for his homosexuality. It's actually a fun read, believe it or not. The first line is "I was 18 years old when I learned to fart." While funny on the surface, his point is that farts are bad and the best little boy in the world is never bad so he never farted. Boggles the mind how he held it in that long; I can barely make it through a couple of hours while we're recording an episode of the podcast without breaking wind.

That book is specifically referenced as the inspiration for a study that came out in the journal *Basic and Applied Social Psychology* in 2013, 40 years after that fartless author wrote it. Titled "The Social Development of Contingent Self-Worth in Sexual Minority Young Men: An Empirical Investigation of the 'Best Little Boy in the World' Hypothesis," the authors tried to measure whether there was anything to this idea that gays are overachievers.[44]

Their findings? Yup. Gays "cope with early stigma by strongly investing in achievement-related success" compared to their straight counterparts. Not only that, they do so to their own detriment. The study also found that "investment in achievement-related domains exacts negative health consequences for young sexual minority men." In other words, gays are capable of overachieving so hard they'll make themselves sick or injure themselves.

> **Mike:** *My guess is that overachievers will always exist, that it'll always be because they're trying to fill a hole.*
>
> **Kyle:** *Boy, I've been trying to fill a hole for so much of my life, Mike.*
>
> **EPISODE 348: OVERACHIEVING**

In this study, these boys realize that they are attracted to other boys, on average, at the age of 11. The average age these boys came out of the closet is 16-and-a-half. These ages are consistently seen in various studies, with the usual being an awareness of same-sex attraction at an average of 10 years and coming out of the closet at an average of age 17. Those seven years, the "I know I'm gay but I'm hiding it" years, have a profound impact on development. A quick personal aside, I knew I was into other boys around 11 or so, yet didn't come out until I was 30. Even though my gap is far wider than the average pointed to in the study, it's comforting to know that I'm not the only one, by a long shot, that had to go through the "I know I'm gay but I'm hiding it years."

The study postulates that "besting others at competitive tasks represents one way for young sexual minority men to control a threatening environment, although not without cost." This idea that it is ultimately about control is super interesting. You can't control your sexual orientation; we've seen that over and over again. So, to compensate, we control what we can.

So, the case is closed, right?

Well, not exactly. First, there are other kinds of achievement out there than a perfect GPA. There are tons of awards to win, positions to hold, money to be made, beautiful people to bang, and sports to dominate. Even if gay boys are more invested in competition, one of the theories the study puts forth as to why they found what they found, GPA isn't necessarily what they'll invest in.

Second, and perhaps more importantly, despite the "best little boy in the world" phenomenon, LGBT people as a population have a hard time with school. A 2009 study in the *Economics of Education Review* titled "LGBT students: New evidence on demographics and educational outcomes" showed pretty definitively that LGBT students are less likely to graduate, less likely to continue on to college, and have worse academic outcomes (like GPA) than their straight classmates.[45]

It's worth noting that not every LGBTQ+ individual falls into the overachieving stereotype. Take me, for example. I didn't come out of the closet until I was 30, and I certainly wasn't the "best little boy in the world" by any academic measure. In fact, I struggled with ADHD, which made it challenging to conform to the highest academic standards society often places on us. That diagnosis was such an "aha" moment for me. Suddenly my undergraduate pattern of 3.7 one quarter followed by 2.6 the next made sense.

Despite my highly inconsistent GPA, I do have a problem with perfectionism. I'm my own worst enema. Sorry, I mean enemy. I find myself valuing my accomplishments less than I should. I tend to focus on the gap between where I'm at and where I think perfection is. A lot of therapy has shown me that some part of me feels deeply unworthy.

Striving for an elusive perfection is a thread that connects a lot of us in the queer community. Whether through academics, the arts, sports, or simply in our everyday lives, the underlying desire to prove ourselves often remains constant. It is resilience and strength that comes from overcoming adversity and seeking self-acceptance in a world that doesn't always offer it freely.

Whether we conform to the overachieving stereotype or not, we are all worthy of love, acceptance, and celebration just as we are. "Love yourself like your life depends on it, because it does" goes the saying. Or something like that. I don't know, sounds like something a drag queen would say, but she's right.

If the overachieving gay doesn't learn how to love themselves, their story can be bittersweet. While there is a lot to admire in the impressive results they're capable of, there is a certain self-destructiveness to it that can get out of control if the true problem of feeling "enough" isn't addressed. Especially after someone comes out and their shell of overcompensation cracks open.

> **Kyle:** *Productivity is not your worth. That's a hard thing to unpack and dismantle.*
>
> **EPISODE 348: OVERACHIEVING**

So, what happened to J?

I'm not sure that J is even alive. If I remember correctly. he failed out of college. I definitely remember he struggled with alcohol. He tended bar at a male full-frontal strip club for many years, and then he completely disappeared. His clearly abusive boyfriend had influenced him to a life of drugs. They were living on the streets for a while, but eventually even his family lost touch with him. I remember walking the streets of Portland looking for him, wondering if I'd even recognize him if I stumbled upon him. I wish he had listened to that drag queen I probably made up and loved himself like his life depended on it, because it did.

So, is the stereotype true?

The "best little boy in the world" hypothesis has been studied and although there is some nuance it is a phenomenon seen often enough that there is definitely something to it. Whether it takes the form of a 4.0 GPA, a competitiveness on the field or stage, or some other kind of achievement, the overachieving gay is real.

What's the final verdict?

True.

SCORING YOUR QUIZ: QUESTION #6

In the quiz (page 14), we asked you your high school GPA. Here's how to score your results:

    a. 4.0, I'm brilliant: 2 gay points (because that makes you the "best little boy in the world")

b. 3.0–3.9: 1 gay point (because that makes you a "pretty good little boy in the world")

c. < 3.0, not an academic powerhouse: 0 gay points

d. 2.5, but I sucked a lot of dicks: 5 gay points (good boy)

You Probably Have Impeccable Taste

What's the stereotype?

Gay men are stylish and have impeccable taste.

Gays are basically like the Fab Five, right?

Gay men are always on trend. They're witty and sophisticated and perfectly dressed. It's assumed that gay men have better fashion sense than straight men, and that we have perfectly decorated homes. And if he's an interior designer, he *must* be gay, right?

Kyle, you often joke that you didn't get the stylish gay gene, right?

I first realized I liked boys around junior high. I came out when I was 19. That means that, for about eight years of my life, I kept a lot of secrets. I didn't just hide my interest in boys; I hid anything that might give away that I could be gay. I kept most of myself locked away tight, hoping no one would find out the truth.

When I came out, it was a first step towards being a more

authentic version of myself, but it didn't immediately change all the lessons I learned: keep to yourself; don't share too much of yourself; don't tell anyone else much about yourself; be who they want you to be, not who you really are. I had to (and continue) to try to break these habits I formed during my formative years.

I don't let too many people in. I'm trying to change that, but I know I'm a harder nut to crack than most. I keep my feelings, opinions, and interests to myself. I'm always worried they may be "wrong" or "stupid" or, yes, "gay."

I don't let too many people into my life, and I mean that physically as well. My condo, the physical space where I'm free to be myself, is something that reveals a lot of who I am, and I've always been terrified to share that with people. Letting people into my space opens me up to judgment. It lets people see the truth of who I am and how I live. What if they hate it? Or worse, laugh at it? What if the way I live repulses them? What if, after learning more about me, they don't like me at all?

Being gay and hiding my true self for so long has made me a ball of anxiety when it comes to letting people in. And, to make it worse, there are the expectations that, because I'm gay, I'll have an immaculately decorated condo.

So, where did all that anxiety come from?

I remember catching an episode or two of *Queer Eye for the Straight Guy* when I was younger and in the closet. Five stylish gay men went around fixing all the straight men, improving their wardrobe and their furnishings. I never identified with the gay men on the show; I always identified with the train wrecks they were trying to fix.

I didn't know how to dress, either. I was never the stylish gay. Even today, my look is often a t-shirt and jeans with flip flops. If you're lucky, I've showered in the past few days (thanks, depression).

It's not just the guys from *Queer Eye for the Straight Guy.* It's Tim Gunn. It's Nate Berkus. It's Marc Jacobs. It's Marc St. James from *Ugly Betty.* It's the new guys from *Queer Eye.* There are plenty of examples of fashionable gay men who know how to decorate, design, and style. It's an expectation of gay men, that we're a good person to invite if you need help interior decorating or need a judgy bitch to help you find the right wardrobe. That has never been me, and it's made me feel even more self-conscious about letting people in.

If we're looking at the design, style, and aesthetic expectations of gay men, it would make sense to take a look at interior decorating as a case study. If we're more

Kyle: *You're very ugh about this topic. Tell me why you're not excited about this.*

Mike: *I'm wearing gym shorts and a t-shirt that says "that's what I do: I drink and I know things" with the Lannister lion on it, and wine stains on it because I poured wine on myself watching Game of Thrones, and you're wearing a marathon t-shirt for a race you did not run in.*

Kyle: *I signed up for it though, which I think deserves recognition.*

EPISODE 115: FASHION

stylish, more of us should be interior decorators, right? A 2019 article[46] in InteriorDesign.net says that "little data exists regarding how many gay men are out in the design industry around the world, but it's without a doubt a friendlier industry than, say, professional sports." Then again, almost any profession will seem gay when you compare it to sports. Another website, Zippia.com, claims[47] that "23% of commercial interior designers are LGBT," based on "a database of 30 million profiles." What database? Where is the data coming from? It's not explained on the site. If the data were accurate, current US estimates of LGBTQ+ people put the number around 7–8%,[48] which would mean there are 3.3 times as many LGBT interior designers as compared to the general population. It's unclear how accurate Zippia.com is as a data source, though, so I'm taking those numbers with a grain of salt.

Even though we can't say conclusively that gay men are overrepresented in interior design, we know that it's stereotyped as such. According to a research study[49] documenting the stereotyping of interior designers, the reason gay men began pursuing interior design is that, after World War II, many gay men refused to return to the small cities they were from now that they had been exposed to what's out there. Instead, they went to cities like New York and San Francisco, and many began working in creative professions, one of which was interior design.

In 1971, then-President Richard Nixon said, in a recorded phone conversation, that, "the upper class in San Francisco is that way. The Bohemian Grove, which I attend from time to time—it is the most faggy goddamned thing you could ever imagine, with that San Francisco crowd. I can't shake hands with anybody from San Francisco. Decorators. They got to do something. But we don't have to glorify it." Even Nixon knew that interior designers were gay.

It's interesting to note that interior designing as a profession is often credited as being created by Elsie de Wolfe, who was openly lesbian. So, a lesbian created a profession that was then predominantly female, which was then seen as acceptable for gay men to work in. Despite this, being gay wasn't always fully accepted in the profession. According to a 2020 article in BusinessOfHome.com, "Forty years ago, you might have seen a lot of gay men's apartments in *Architectural Digest,* but you wouldn't have read about their boyfriends or partners." Apparently, you could be a gay interior designer, but "that fact wasn't always acknowledged in the media—or even, in some cases, by the clients who hired them."

It seems like you're not alone though, Kyle

I'm not the only one who feels the pressure of this stereotype. In a 2023 article on Slate,[50] Rhodes Murphy says, "As a gay man, the cleanliness of my home and tastefulness of its decor have increasingly become sources of anxiety and shame." When the expectations are that you've got impeccable taste, anything less than perfection feels like a failure. So, then, welcoming people into your home is inviting people in to see your failure first-hand. According to the subtitle of the article, Murphy has decided, "I'm done letting the stereotype of the tidy, tasteful homosexual get in the way of my messy, unmanicured joy." There's a chance for all of us to release ourselves from the tasteful expectations that stereotypes have placed on our heads and homes.

A 2017 article on Stuff.co.nz[51] (what's up, kiwis!) proclaims in its title that "Not all gay men are interiors experts." In it, author Lee Suckling explains that he knows gays who don't have their shit together when it comes to interior decorating. "I can't tell you how many friends' homes I've walked into only to discover futon couches and football flags hanging from the walls—the same stuff you'd find in the flat of a group of straight blokes." Not only does Suckling dismiss this stereotype as untrue, he calls it "a harmful generalisation; one rooted in misogyny." The assumption is that women are the ones that are responsible for taking care of the home, therefore it's a feminine interest, therefore it's associated with gays.

Yet another article, written by Adam Lusher in the *Independent* in 2016,[52] is titled, "Stereotyping gay men as stylish and witty 'prevents people seeing them as proper individuals'." I think it's true that, if all you see are your expectations of gay men, you don't get to know the true person underneath. You see only what you want to see. Or worse, you see only what that gay man can offer you—style and class—rather than see him as the whole (hole?) person who has flaws, just like the rest of the world. In the article, Lusher interviews a researcher, Ashley Brooks, who indicates that, because these stereotypes are seen as positive ones (who wouldn't want to be an amazing interior decorator, right?), people are less likely to push back on them, "despite their potential to cause long-term damage." The last line of the article is my favorite. It quotes novelist Paul Burston as saying, "Some gay men are very, very boring and very badly dressed." It's true. We don't all fit into a neat package based on expectations delivered to us from the media.

Speaking of being poorly dressed, what about another industry where we'd expect to see the stereotype show up—fashion? Similar to interior decorators, *The Washington Post* said in a 2013 article that, "There are no statistics about the numbers of gay men in the fashion industry."[53] The article does, however, acknowledge that "The stereotype of the gay designer is so deeply ingrained in the culture that it is often assumed to be a fact. Whether industry insider or casual observer, people often presume that a male designer is gay until he announces himself otherwise." This assumption of gayness, like in interior design, is deeply ingrained in our public consciousness, and it doesn't seem that any data is there to confirm or deny.

Enter, yet again, our friends at Zippia.com who claim that "18% of all fashion designers are LGBT." This would be more than double the current estimates of LGBT people in the population, meaning this career also over-indexes for LGBT people. But again, their sources remain elusive to me, so I won't rest my laurels on them.

A 2006 article on *ABC News* titled "Gay Stereotypes: Are They True?"[54] interviews Ted Allen, one of the original cast members of *Queer Eye for the Straight Guy,* who acknowledges that, "Not all gay men are superstylish. Not all straight men are bad dressers." Also, according to the article, there's research that shows that gay men are more likely to prefer "fashion, interior design and hair coloring," but they don't name a source on this, so again, tangible data is limited.

Limited, but not nonexistent?

The tangible data I was able to find came from a research paper titled "Queer Eye for the Straight Guy: Sexual Orientation and Stereotype Lift Effects on Performance in the Fashion Domain."[55] In it, researchers wanted to know if gay men outperformed straight men on a quiz of fashion knowledge. However, there's a catch: for some of the participants (the test group), they were asked to fill out a demographic survey, including their sexual orientation, *before* taking the quiz. They were also told that the researchers were evaluating their "natural fashion sense." (The control group filled out the demographic info after, and they were not given the note about "natural fashion sense.") The intention was to evaluate whether reminding gays of the stereotype, that they are supposed to be better at fashion, would impact their scores. They defined this as a "stereotype lift," or "a boost in performance caused by an awareness of a positive ingroup stereotype."

The results? Gay men outperformed straight men on the fashion quiz, but only for the tested group who were, in fact, reminded about the supposedly positive stereotype about their fashion sense. Those in the control group performed equally, whether gay or straight. As their paper summarizes, "This pattern of results suggests that the superior performance of gay men in the stereotype salient condition was a result of stereotype lift, rather than inherent group differences." In other words, the better performance wasn't a result of inherent differences between gays and straights, but rather due to this "stereotype lift."

My takeaway from this study is that stereotypes have a real impact on our day-to-day lives. The assumption that we're all impeccably dressed and have immaculate homes is pervasive; it's impossible to hide from. As a result, we're under constant pressure to "outperform" our straight counterparts on fashion knowledge, forcing us to live up to a stereotype that not all of us see ourselves in. No wonder there are so many articles railing against this one—we're being held captive by some ghost of perfect taste that we never wanted to have to live up to.

Much to my chagrin, I don't think I've been affected by the stereotype lift. I'm aware the stereotype of the gay man with impeccable taste exists, but I don't think it's done anything to improve my fashion or design knowledge.

When you are in the closet, there are a lot of assumptions that are being made about you regularly, primarily that of straightness. I suppose it's not just an assumption because there were multiple times when I was questioned, perhaps interrogated, by schoolmates as to whether I was gay. Another time, my dad questioned my super-duper gay browsing history. In all these instances, I relentlessly defended my straightness, as if I were offended by any other implication.

Once I came out, I eschewed the presumption of straightness and was able to take a step toward being my more authentic self. However, what I didn't realize at the time, was that there were still plenty of assumptions that were made about me and what it meant to be gay. Again, maybe it's not fair to define them as assumptions because I played into them. I pretended I liked and cared about fashion. I watched E!'s *Fashion Police,* trying to glean some sort of knowledge from it that I could apply to my regular life. I tried being bitchy about others' fashion choices and pretended I cared when celebrities wore a horrendous outfit.

Really, I was just buying into a whole new set of stereotypes that existed purely because I was gay. And the fact that I didn't know a thing about fashion or how to decorate only meant that I felt imposter syndrome any time I was around truly fashionable gays. I even got down on myself when particularly well-dressed straight men were in my orbit. How was I such a bad gay that even straight men can outdo me? Where's my stereotype lift, giving me some sort of boost to my knowledge just by being made aware of the existence of the stereotype?

As I've gotten older, I've tried to move beyond the assumptions of who I'm supposed to be just because I'm gay. I've tried to embrace the clothes that I wear, even if they aren't the most fashionable. I feel comfortable in a t-shirt and jeans, and that's OK. Every now and then, I'll find something unique, like a purple jacket or a Britney t-shirt that speaks to me, and I'll wear it without the expectation that it's a new trend or that I'm making a fashion statement. I just like what I like, and that's OK.

I've also started to let more people in, both physically and emotionally. I've come to realize that—stereotypes and assumptions aside—I like who I am as a person. I'm interesting and funny and creative and empathetic and obviously humble (obviously). My condo doesn't have to look like the after on a home makeover show. It can be whatever I want it to be. (Interjection from Mike: I actually think his condo is pretty cute.) My style doesn't have to fit with the stereotype of the impeccable gay style, it can just be mine. And, with that, letting people into my home and into my heart is a healthy way to love the person I am, just the way I am.

So, is the stereotype true?

From homes styling to fashion sense, gays are expected to have better taste than straight people. Even Nixon knew that there was something gay about being an interior designer. Anecdotally, it does seem to be true that gay men are more likely to work in the fashion and decorating industries. Plus, if Zippia.com is to be believed, there are hard numbers confirming we're overrepresented in those fields. Plus, there's at least one study showing that gays do outperform straight men on a fashion test, but only when reminded about the stereotype that gays are better at fashion. In the real world, with shows like *Queer Eye for the Straight Guy*, it's hard to avoid the reminder that we're expected to have better style. There's no hard and fast data that can confirm this stereotype without a shadow of a doubt, but all the information I could find says that there's something to this stereotype.

What's the final verdict?

Somewhat true.

SCORING YOUR QUIZ: QUESTION #7

In the quiz (page 14), we asked you where your furniture is from. Here's how to score your results:

a. Pottery Barn, Crate & Barrel, and West Elm: 2 gay points
b. Target, Ikea, and the thrift shop: 1 gay point
c. Wal-Mart, Craigslist, and from when my brother moved out: 0 gay points

8

You're Probably a Pedophile

What's the stereotype?

LGBTQ+ people, particularly gay men, are pedophiles.

eye roll I've heard that one before.

Yeah, this is an old one that's hard to shake. Some people believe that gay men are a danger to children. Whether it's calling us "pedophiles" or "groomers," people assume that we "recruit" young people to join our gay brigade. And it has been going on for a while.

So, where did it come from, Kyle?

Why do some people associate homosexuality with pedophilia? Yes, it's partially because they're assholes. But it's not arbitrary. This connection didn't pop out of thin air. It came from somewhere. And at least in the modern times, it goes back to McCarthyism.

I didn't pay a lot of attention in history class, so I hate to have to be the one to explain McCarthyism to you, but here we go. During the 1940s and 50s, Senator Joseph McCarthy led a campaign to find and root out communists from the government. As it turns out, this was a scare tactic built on false accusations as a way to spread fear in the country (i.e. the "Red Scare") and persecute left-wingers.

What I didn't learn in high school was that there was a similar Lavender Scare, meaning gays were also targeted. McCarthy is quoted as saying: "If you want to be against McCarthy, boys, you've got to be either a Communist or a cocksucker."[56] (I came here to either be a communist or suck some cock, and I'm all out of communism.) In 1950, Congress began investigating the government for gays. The theory was that, if you're gay, you're more likely to be targeted by foreign governments and blackmailed because of the threat of your gay identity being revealed to the public. As a result of the Lavender Scare, at least 425 people were fired from the government due to allegations of homosexuality.

OK, but I thought this was about pedophilia.

I know. None of this has anything to do with pedophilia quite yet. The point is, this was a major period in time where people were riled up about the threat of gay people to society. The Lavender Scare ignited fear of homosexuality, and it wasn't long before this fear spread to other places.

In 1956, the Florida legislature formed the Florida Legislative Investigation Committee, referred to as the Johns Committee. Yes, everything bad starts in Florida. Originally, the Johns Committee was "born out of opposition to the desegregation of schools and the pursuit of 'communists.'"[57] After running into roadblocks when trying to target the NAACP and communists, they turned their sights on the gays in 1958. More specifically, they started investigating gays in schools, believing gay teachers to be a danger to students.

By 1963, as a result of the Johns Committee's investigation into homosexuality in schools, 39 professors and faculty members had been fired, 71 teaching certificates had been revoked, and "scores" of students were expelled from public colleges.[58]

"Homosexuals are dangerous as teachers or youth leaders because they try to get sexually involved with children." In a 1970 national survey, 70% of Americans agreed with this statement.[59] These kinds of mass hysterias, like the Johns Committee, don't just impact the individuals who were fired, expelled, or died by suicide as a result of the allegations. I believe that they are the reason society has locked into its public consciousness the association of gays as a danger to children.

In 1977, Dade County, Florida passed an ordinance that offered protection in housing and employment to gays. A major victory! We celebrated, and everyone was happy. Just kidding. There was a huge backlash against it. One of the vocal opponents was Anita Bryant. She was already a public figure because she had three Top 20 hits, was Miss Oklahoma, and was seen on commercials for Florida orange juice. She spearheaded the "Save Our Children" campaign against the ordinance, protesting, among other things, that this protection in employment meant that openly gay teachers were protected.

One of her arguments was that "homosexuals cannot reproduce, so they must recruit. And to freshen their ranks, they must recruit the youth of America."[60] This is that connection that anti-gay people will strike up between gays and the danger to young people. It's the same foundation as the fear that gays are pedophiles: that we can't be trusted around children. And her fearmongering worked; as a result of her efforts, the ordinance was repealed with 69% of the vote.

As a side note, Anita Bryant is well known for getting a pie to the face during a news conference in 1977. Annoyingly, she started praying for the person that pied her. But still, we stand with pie-based activism.

OK, but what does the research say?

The 70s were also when actual scientific research began to address the question of a connection between homosexuality and pedophilia. In 1978, in what may be the first research study of its kind, Groth and Birnbaum published "Adult sexual orientation and attraction to underage persons." They looked at a random sample of 175 men convicted of sexually assaulting children. Their findings? "The possibility emerges [...] that the adult heterosexual male constitutes a greater risk to the underage child than does the adult homosexual male."[61] So, if you're worried about the safety of children, be wary of straight men, not gay men.

Unfortunately, there were studies that claimed otherwise. For example, a 1988 study called "Behavior patterns of child molesters" was published in the *Archives of Sexual Behavior*. It states that, "Eighty-six percent of offenders against males described themselves as homosexual or bisexual."[62] However, this off-handed assertion isn't supported with any tangible explanation. In one critique, Dr. Herek, "an internationally recognized authority on prejudice against sexual minorities," according to his own website[63] (hey, I love a doctor with self-confidence), says, "no details are provided about how this information was ascertained, making it difficult to interpret or evaluate." Science should detail how and where its data comes from, and this 86% number doesn't do that. Unfortunately, you'll still see people quote this statistic as fact rather than the anomaly that it is.

There are plenty of other studies that have looked into this. There was a study in 1989 that found that "homosexual males who preferred mature partners responded no more to male children than heterosexual males who preferred mature partners responded to female children."[64] In layman's terms, gays are no more likely to be pedophiles than straights. A 1994 study found that, out of 269 cases studied, "two offenders were identified as being gay or lesbian."[65]

A 2005 publication called "Lesbian and Gay Parenting" by the American Psychological Association states that "available evidence reveals that gay men are no more likely than heterosexual men to perpetrate child sexual abuse."[66] In 2009, a study commissioned by the US Catholic Bishops (!!!) found that "we do not find a connection between homosexual identity and the increased likelihood of subsequent abuse from the data that we have right now."[67] Reputable sources clearly state that gays are not more likely to be pedophiles.

Unfortunately, one source of misinformation has been a 2002 article by Timothy J. Dailey called "Homosexuality and Child Abuse" published by the Family Research Council (FRC), an anti-LGBTQ+ think tank. This article claims that scientific research supports their assertion that homosexuality and pedophilia are linked. It's important to know that the paper has been taken down from the FRC's website. Exactly when this happened, I can't be sure, but it was up long enough for conservative circles to continue to use its talking points. The article was one of those that looks legit because of all the references to studies and research it contains. But, just because something has footnotes/endnotes doesn't mean it's the truth. (I recognize I'm saying this after using at least 12 endnotes in this chapter so far, but I still mean it.) A lot of the studies I've mentioned are included as endnotes. Some, like that 1988 study, don't hold up to scrutiny. Other studies prove exactly the opposite of what Dailey is claiming. In fact, there's a full breakdown of the issues with Dailey's article on the self-confident doctor's blog,[68] which I suggest you read if you want the full scoop.

Another issue that makes it seem like gay pedophiles are common is the terminology we use. Many people will describe instances of a male molesting a male child as "homosexual." However, the sexual orientation of a person is decided based on the adults they are attracted to. Many male pedophiles who molested boys are self-identified straight men with wives and kids. So, to label what they did as "homosexual" is misleading at best and downright offensive at worst. Instead, Dr. Herek suggests that we use male-male molestation (rather than "homosexual") so as not to make any undue assumptions about the orientation of the perpetrator. The way we talk about things matters.

Speaking of how we talk about things, there's been a recent resurgence in right-wingers calling us pedophiles, often using a shiny new term: "groomer." Not only is this kind of language harmful to LGBTQ+ people, but it affects our ability to effectively talk about the very real issue of grooming.

Wait... "groomer" means a thing that's not the thing that they think it means?

Grooming is a term that refers to "manipulative behaviors that the abuser uses to gain access to a potential victim, coerce them to agree to the abuse, and reduce the risk of being caught."[69] This may include things like isolating their victim physically or emotionally, building trust with them, teaching them to keep secrets (so they keep the relationship a secret), and trying to normalize increasingly sexual contact. It's an important term that has a meaning, and diluting that meaning can make it harder to understand true child predatory behaviors.

According to the Anti-Defamation League, the leading anti-hate organization in the world, the far-right and extremists "launched a significant attack against the LGBTQ+ community in 2021–2022" by claiming that LGBTQ+ people are "groomers." It's the same old attacks against our community, only with a fresh new word.

As attacks against our community escalated, in March 2022, the "Don't Say Gay" bill (more accurately known as the Parental Rights in Education Act) was signed into law by Gayish Award-winning Dickbag Fuckface Asshole of the Year for 2023[70] Ron DeSantis. See?

Everything bad *still* starts in Florida. These bills, on their surface, may seem harmless, advocating for age-appropriate discussions of sexual orientation and gender issues. But, in fact, it attempts to re-move educators' ability to discuss LGBTQ+ issues at all. It also rein-forces that idea that Anita Bryant tried to push all those years ago, that teachers are trying to recruit or indoctrinate kids.

While I personally thought we had seen more forward progress on this stereotype, that it had become very clear that gays aren't pedophiles, the unfortunate truth is that it's still being used as an attack launched at LGBTQ+ people as a whole. I only wish those that attacked us could read and understand scientific studies so that they would know that gays aren't, in fact, more likely to be pedophiles.

So, is the stereotype true?

There is no way, under any circumstances, that this stereotype is true. Often-quoted statistics, such as the 86% number, don't hold up to scrutiny, even though it still is used by those that want to pretend to have an intelligent argument. Whether it's pedophile or groomer, this is a stereotype that, unfortunately, still persists. Here's hoping that someday, everyone will finally realize that LGBTQ+ people are not more likely to be pedophiles.

What's the final verdict?

False.

SCORING YOUR QUIZ: QUESTION #8

In the quiz (page 14), we asked if you're a threat to children. Here's how to score your results:

a. Yes, I am: -1 gay point (because, at least according to one study, this means you're more likely to be straight)

b. Yes, but just the altar boys: 0 gay points (but you get 1000 Catholic Priest points)

c. Yes, but only if they ruin my flight to Palm Springs: 1 gay point

d. No: 0 gay points (because, in truth, these things have nothing to do with each other)

9

You Probably Watch *The Golden Girls*

What's the stereotype?

Gays love *The Golden Girls*.

Picture it. Sicily. 1912.

The Golden Girls is a classic sitcom that gays love. I don't know what more to say. They just do.

So, is the stereotype true?

Yup.

What's the final verdict?

100% true.

SCORING YOUR QUIZ: QUESTION #9

In the quiz (page 14), we asked how many episodes of *The Golden Girls* you've watched. Here's how to score your results:

a. 0: 0 gay points

b. 1–4: 1 gay point

c. 5–179: 2 gay points

d. All 180 and *The Golden Palace*, too: 5 gay points

10

You're Probably a Flight Attendant, Hairdresser, or Nurse

What's the stereotype?

Gay men are more likely to be flight attendants, hairdressers, and nurses.

Flight attendants and hairdressers and nurses, oh my!

There are certain professions that just seem to attract more gay men than straight. It's assumed in jobs like flight attendants, hairdressers, and nurses that, if you're male, you're probably gay. Maybe people make the assumption because they're female-dominated professions. Maybe it's because they're customer service-focused jobs. But are the men in these professions really more likely to be gay? What types of jobs are gay men drawn to, and why?

OK, Kyle, you usually have the gayta. Lay it on me.

I shuffle in line, holding my two carry-ons, slowly making progress towards the open door of the aircraft. One by one, the people ahead of me duck into the plane until finally, it's my turn. I see the cute flight attendant. He smiles at me and says, "Welcome!" I smile back and then make my way down the aisle towards my seat. All the while, I'm thinking to myself, "He must be gay."

I'm embarrassed to admit that I sometimes reflexively succumb to believing in stereotypes. The idea that all male flight attendants are gay is a big one, and it's hard for me to shake. I know working in a specific profession doesn't make someone gay. I know straight male flight attendants exist. I know that I can't tell someone's orientation just by looking at them (see Chapter 14 about gaydar). But still, it's a hard stereotype to fight.

I'm most assuredly not the first person to point out that there are certain jobs that seem to attract gay men. Not only that, but apparently it goes back further than I realized. In his 1897 book, *Sexual Inversion,* physician Havelock Ellis noticed that gay men tended to gravitate towards certain disciplines, like acting, literature, medicine, and hairdressing. Yup. Since at least as early as 1897, we've been looking at hairdressers and thinking, "that boy gay" (note: not a direct quote from Ellis).

At the same time, Ellis acknowledged that this was a generalization and that gay people could work in other fields. He said, "no class of occupation furnishes a safeguard"[71] against gay people. Despite the negative slant of that quote, the book was progressive for its time given, according to Wikipedia, "he did not characterise [homosexuality] as a disease, immoral, or a crime."[72] Hoo-fucking-ray. Then again, he was also a eugenicist, so we don't need to ring the celebration bells too loudly for him.

The observation Ellis made about gay professions is still being studied today, albeit with a little more rigor and depth in the research practices. For example, while society has strong associations with what professions attract gay men, the same is true for lesbians, who are often stereotyped as gym coaches or mechanics. What types of jobs are they attracted to? And are there any explanations as to why gays and lesbians are attracted to certain jobs? A 2015 study, called "Concealable Stigma and Occupational Segregation: Toward a Theory of Gay and Lesbian Occupations,"[73] aimed to answer those questions.

It's just that thing where gay men do feminine things, yeah?

Some people may believe that the answer is an easy one: gay men are drawn to stereotypically feminine professions (e.g. flight attendant), and lesbians are drawn to stereotypically masculine professions (e.g. mechanic). According to the study, it's true that gay men *are* in fact more likely to be in female-dominated occupations than are heterosexual men, and lesbians *are* more likely to be in male-dominated occupations than are heterosexual women. But it doesn't explain the full picture. The researchers reviewed US data and found that "nearly half of gay men are actually in occupations in which men are the majority of workers, and two-thirds of lesbians work in female-majority occupations." Gay men don't exclusively work in female-dominated professions, nor do lesbians in male-dominated ones. Clearly there's something more going on here.

This study hypothesizes that the "something more" going on is that gay people prioritize two qualities in our jobs: *task independence* and *social perceptiveness*. Task independence is defined as the "freedom to perform one's tasks without substantially depending on others," and social perceptiveness is the "accurate anticipation and reading of others' reactions." Together, the study's authors theorize these two qualities can explain what types of jobs gays and lesbians gravitate towards.

And the research shows their hypothesis is true. After analyzing data from the US Census Bureau's American Community Survey and the US National Longitudinal Study of Adolescent Health, they found that "both task independence and social perceptiveness have a positive, significant relationship to the proportion of gay or lesbian workers in an occupation." Gays and lesbians are, in fact, over-represented in jobs that offer either task independence, social perceptiveness, or both.

To understand why, researchers viewed these two qualities through the lens of "concealable stigma." Unlike some other minority groups, LGBTQ+ people can (to some extent) conceal their minority status by not disclosing their sexual orientation or gender identity, which may be done to avoid the potential negative stigma of society. Coming out is not a one-time event; it's an on-going decision that has to be made time and time again based on the person, situation, and environment.

Concealable stigma might explain why we want a job with *task independence.* One way we can deal with the possible stigma we'd face if we came out to coworkers is to find jobs that rely less on our coworkers to begin with. The research paper gives examples of task-independent jobs, including massage therapists or taxi drivers. These don't rely on coworkers or bosses as much as others, and therefore we are less likely to be forced to disclose our sexual orientation, which may lessen the stigma we have to put up with at our job.

It's a weird feeling knowing that concealing our identities due to societal stigma might have made us care more about the ability to work independently at our jobs. I suspect we may be more likely to value independence beyond just professionally, too. It reminds me of feeling excluded on the playground because I would rather be playing with the girls than the boys. It reminds me of drifting away from my high school best friend after I came out because I didn't want to face her and the fact that I had spent so much time lying to her. It reminds me of being a single gay man without a partner, living alone, learning to be happy with just myself. There's a feeling of isolation that comes along with being in the closet growing up, and I wonder if we hold on to that isolation in the work we seek out to avoid what we fear: being judged by others.

The other skill researchers suggest that we prioritize is *social perceptiveness.* Growing up gay and in the closet requires hyper-vigilance. We're ever watchful of other people to see how they react to us, to see if they suspect anything, and to keep our cover. As a result, we may have an above-average ability to perceive social cues, a skill that is much needed in some professions. As stated in the paper, "awareness and anticipation of others' reactions and mental states—whether they are patients in a healthcare setting, passengers on a plane, audience members in a theater, or students in a classroom—are relatively important components of many such jobs." The watchful eye we grew up with can translate into a useful professional skill, in the right job.

It seems like concealable stigma might have given me some of this superpower of social perceptiveness. While it's based on the frustrating need to monitor both my own and others' behaviors very closely, maybe it's also given me a special ability to be in tune with others' feelings and needs, making me better at certain jobs that involve taking care of others. It reminds me of how I've been described as "one of the most empathic people I know" by one of my former bosses. It reminds me of how the men I've dated describe how sensitive I am to their needs. It reminds me of how much I care about the thoughts and opinions of other people. I think it's made me a better friend and partner. And it might make me better at certain jobs.

And now, the fun part. The research identified specific jobs that over-index in gays and lesbians. Yes, we know the specific jobs that gays and lesbians are most likely to hold. They broke the jobs down into subcategories based on whether the occupation was a female-majority or male-majority occupation.

For gay men working in female-majority occupations, the top three jobs are:

1. flight attendants
2. hairdressers, hairstylists, and cosmetologists
3. nurse practitioners.

This list seems to suggest that the stereotypes we have of gay men's professions are true. My assumption that the male flight attendant smiling as I board the plane is gay may not be 100% accurate, but it's based on a kernel of truth, at least according to this study's findings.

However, remember that gay men don't just work in female-dominated jobs. The top three jobs that gay men over-indexed for *within male-dominated professions* are:

1. actors
2. news analysts, reporters, and correspondents
3. artists and related workers.

Looks like gay men really do love the creative professions!

Similar lists were established for lesbians. The top jobs for lesbians in male-dominated professions are:

1. bus and truck mechanics and diesel engine specialists
2. elevator installers/repairers
3. heating, A/C, and refrigeration mechanics/installers.

I guess the stereotype that lesbians are good with heavy machinery and appliances is based on truth, given these professions.

But, just like gay men, lesbians don't only work in male-majority professions. The top jobs lesbians have *within female-dominated professions* are:

1. psychologists
2. probation officers/correctional treatment specialists
3. training and development specialists and managers.

A less stereotypical list, if you ask me.

There's a couple of surprises in there though, yeah?

As I look across these various jobs that are more likely to be held by gays or lesbians, some feel extremely stereotypical, like the fact that gays are more likely to be flight attendants. But others are surprising, like that lesbians are more likely to be psychologists. The professions that stand out in our heads as stereotypical only account for some of the actual gay jobs. This study helps to clarify that these other, less stereotypical jobs can be explained because they require those skills that we excel at: task independence or social perceptiveness (or both).

Because these skills are borne of concealable stigma, the research paper points out that they may become obsolete as acceptance of LGBTQ+ people grows. The more accepting people are of gays, the less we're required to conceal our identities, and the less importance we may place on jobs that require task independence and social perceptiveness. I hope, one day, there's a future where the research shows that there aren't any jobs that are more or less likely to be home to gays and lesbians, and that we're all equally likely to work in any profession. If we ever get to that point, it could mean we're finally to a place where we're all treated and behave the same, not forged by the stigma we face.

I don't foresee that happening any time soon, though, especially considering we've been noticing that gays flock to certain professions since at least 1897. I think straight men in particular would have to unlearn a lot of sexism and gender norms in order to be OK with working at a female-majority profession, much less a job that's stereotyped as being a heavily gay job.

Also, once gay men see that certain professions, like flight attendants, are more likely to be accepting of them, it's a self-fueling stereotype. More gays are likely to work there because more gays already work there. Not to mention the idea that people get jobs based on connections and referrals, and gay people would be more likely to have gay friends that they would refer to their professions.

So, as I continue down the aisle, I keep thinking of that cute flight attendant. I stow my larger carry-on item, get situated in my seat, and quickly pop in my headphones so that the people sitting in my row know that I am *not* a talker. Then, I check Scruff to see if I can find the cute flight attendant in my grid. I know it's an assumption I made based on stereotypes, but hey, some stereotypes just seem to fit. Fingers crossed that I find him.

So, is the stereotype true?

At least one research study shows rather directly that the stereotype is true: gay men are more likely to be flight attendants, hairdressers, and nurses. This is, of course, only part of the puzzle. Gay men can work in just about any job or profession. In fact, nearly half of gay men work in male-dominated professions. The variables that come into play seem to be task independence and social perceptiveness, which may help explain why gays have the types of jobs that they do. But, still, when we look at the list of top jobs for gay men within female-dominated professions, it's flight attendants, hairdressers, and nurses, just like you might expect.

What's the final verdict?

True.

SCORING YOUR QUIZ: QUESTION #10

In the quiz (page 14), we asked you your profession. Here's how to score your results:

- **a.** Flight attendant: 2 gay points
- **b.** Nurse: 2 gay points
- **c.** Hairdresser: 2 gay points
- **d.** None of the above, but something equally gay: 2 gay points
- **e.** None of the above: 0 gay points

11

You've Probably Never Touched a Vagina

What's the stereotype?

The gayer you are, at least if you're a man, the more repulsed you are by vaginas.

This is that "Gold Star Gay" thing, yeah?

True story. It seems inevitable that any given group of gay men at some point in time will talk about their status, or lack thereof, as a "Gold Star Gay." There is no getting around the crude meaning: "I have never put my penis in a vagina." There's even "Platinum Star Gay," meaning "I was born by Caesarian section, so I've never even *touched* a vagina."

Kyle: *Before we get into our topic...*

Mike: *Before we get into vaginas?*

Kyle: *Before we dive into vaginas...*

Mike: *I'm terrified of this topic. We're gonna fuck it up. Neither of us have a vagina. I have some experience with one. It did not go well.*

EPISODE 093: VAGINAS

So, what does that make you, Mike?

If the glamorous labels for not interacting with a vagina are gold and platinum, I'm fond of saying I'm a "Lead Star Gay." Lead is a metal that is dull, heavy, malleable, and toxic to the touch. Just like me. The thing is, I was married to a woman for a long time, and we had plenty of sex. When people find out about her, they often ask me if I identify as bisexual (I do not) or when I knew I was gay (about age 11, but I married her anyway). If they're handing out gold medals like some kind of Olympics for faggots, I'm definitely nowhere near the podium. When I was out on the track I knocked down too many of the hurdles instead of jumping over them.

Now, if we pretend all of these precious metal-based ratings are all just good harmless lighthearted fun, I think my little joke about lead is funny, too. Lord knows I've said it at parties and gotten a chuckle. Calling myself out as being made of lead is self-effacing while making a commentary on the validity of the premise. But I've gotta be honest, when I make that joke it's also a defense mechanism. The implication that I'm somehow less than because I have an ex-wife or have on occasion hooked up with trans guys is hurtful. Meant as a harmless joke or not, it really does hurt my feelings. So I joke about it. I wish I didn't have to.

Why are we like this?

Why are we so enamored with the idea that one single vaginal encounter is a mark on your permanent gay record? The whole thing reminds me of another joke that has been told in my family for years now. It takes place in Scotland, so it's best if you read it out loud with an accent, obvi.

A man walks into a bar in Scotland, sits down, and orders a shot of whisky. The American next to him at the bar says, "Howdy, stranger! I'm new to town. The name's Davidson, what's yours?" He's surprised when the man grunts in irritation and scowls, so he asks "Is there something the matter?"

The Scotsman pounds his shot, motions that he'd appreciate another one, and replies "Aye lad, indeed there is something wrong. You see this bar here? I made this bar with me own two hands, slowly crafting it in the time-honored way of my forebears. It took me months to build this bar, but do they call me MacGregor the bar-builder? Noooooo.

"And do you recall the livery stable you passed on the way into town? I stood that stable up in six months, with nary a bit o' help. To this day, that stable is one of the finest in all of Scotland. But do they call me MacGregor the stable-maker? Nooooooo.

"You know the dock your ferry landed at last night? I built that dock with me own two hands, finely honing each joint so that it would withstand the weather that mother nature unravels upon it. I had to swim, with the timbers in me teeth, to build that dock. It took over a year, but do they call me MacGregor the dock-builder? Noooooo.

"You fuck one goat..."

He's MacGregor the Goatfucker now!! Hilarious!

Yes, it's hilarious, especially when told by a good storyteller that can do accents. But it also points to a weird human tendency to believe that a singular experience can somehow irrevocably taint a person. It's the very foundation of the pernicious Christian purity culture. All this brouhaha about virginity and when you lose it and who you lose it to and whether Jesus or Santa were watching you when it happened is only meaningful if we consider virginity to be a precious commodity that can be lost in the first place. I remember losing mine (to a woman, btw) and then laughing the next day at how I didn't feel radically transformed at all. It's just not as big of a deal as we've made it out to be. And we're lucky we live in a fairly secular and permissive society. I'm reminded of the fact that hymen repair surgery is a thing, since having yours damaged or broken, even if not from sex, means you're less desirable as a bride in some cultures.

I assumed that all of this "Gold Star Gay" stuff was a concoction made of one part purity culture, one part misogyny, and one part crude humor. When it comes to misogyny, gay men are capable of some of the worst kinds of woman hating. Perez Hilton basically launched his career being nasty to women. Back in 2014, Rose Mc-Gowan caused quite a stir when she blasted gay men for not standing up more for women's rights and said they are "as misogynistic as straight men, if not more so." I listen to the deafening silence from the gay male community as the US slowly dismantles reproductive rights now that *Roe v. Wade* has been struck down by the Supreme Court, and I can't help but think Rose is on to something. Misogyny is so deep in the gay community I figured "Gold Star Gay" must have been created by us.

Wait, we didn't start it?

As it turns out, gay dudes didn't start it at all! "Gold Star Lesbian" is an even older term. It was originally coined in the US in the early 90s. One of the earliest places it was written down was in a 1995 book *Revolutionary Laughter: A World of Women Comics,* quoting a stand-up act by lesbian comedian Carol Steinel. I'm a little nervous about bringing up the tired old stereotype of the man-hating dyke, but like a lot of stereotypes, there is a kernel of truth in there. Some parts of lesbian culture, especially in the 90s, were indeed anti-penis.

But whether it comes from gay men or lesbians, both camps are guilty of equating genitals and biological sex with gender and there-fore sexual orientation. There are deeply ingrained cisheterosexist attitudes about "boys have a penis and girls have a vagina" and "THERE ARE ONLY TWO GENDERS, PERIOD." These attitudes are factually wrong, but are difficult to shake, even sometimes for those of us in the LGBTQ+ community. This gets combined with a similarly deeply ingrained binary thinking about sexuality, that one has to be completely straight to be valid as a straight man, or completely gay to be valid as a gay man. The same binary thinking goes for the Susan B. Anthony side of the coin as well. (She was a lesbian; look it up!)

This cutesy rating system, when you peel back the surface layers, is all of that sludge mashed together. The laughter makes the whole thing seem innocuous when in actuality it is just, well, offensive. It's offensive to straight women who experimented once in college and now feel permanently altered by the experience. It's offensive to bisexual people, who definitely exist and are perfectly valid even if both the straights and the gays largely either ignore them or sneer at them. It's offensive to cis men who have sex with trans men. It's offensive to trans men who have sex with cis men. It's just offensive and tired, and we should try to stop the joke because it isn't funny anymore.

OK, I'll try to stop... but, first, I have to know, are "Gold Star Gays" the norm?

I'm glad you're going to consider hanging up the medals and retiring the joke about stars and status. But yeah, I was super curious, too, so I looked into it. In 2022, the US Centers for Disease Control and Prevention (CDC) did a survey that covered a lot of different aspects of life, including sexual orientation, gender, and sex. When they asked self-identified gay men about their lifetime sexual experiences and whether they had ever "had sex with a female, ever," 51.4% answered yes. That's over half! Even more pronounced, when they asked self-identified lesbians whether they had ever "had sex with a male, ever," 74.5% said yes. Nearly three quarters.[74]

A quick aside, 87.3% of bi men had ever had sex with a female, and 69.5% had ever had sex with a male. 77.7% with a female and 96.6% with a male for bi women. You'll note that in both cases (not just the women, who seem to always get the credit for sexual fluidity), adding those two percentages is *way* over 100%. It's proof that bisexual people are real and that they really do have sex with both ends of the gender spectrum. It's nice to see a study that cares about bisexuals, too; it can be pretty rare in the literature. We see you, bisexuals![75]

Now we don't know what "had sex with" meant to the people answering the question, so you could argue it doesn't directly address the whole vagina (or penis) based merit badge bullshit. When I finally saw that number, though, I got a little emotional. In cold hard data it says I'm not alone after all. It tells me my experiences definitely don't disqualify me as a gay man. I'm surrounded by Lead Star Gays. If sex with a vagina did somehow mean gay men were somehow suddenly disqualified, half of us would disappear like we got fisted by Thanos's Infinity Gauntlet.

What about all those gays that seem genuinely repulsed?

I'm fond of saying to everyone that you should be into what you're into and not into what you're not. So I'm not going to tell anyone that if they're repulsed by vaginas that they have to suddenly be into vaginas or they're a bad person. I do think, however, if your first reaction to vaginas is disgust, it's important to do a little self-reflection and figure out where that is coming from.

Disgust is a funny thing, and there are lots of different kinds of it. For instance, disgust at seeing or smelling rotten food. Certain animals will evoke disgust in people, like snakes or spiders, and it might even be something that evolved in us for safety reasons (the jury is out on some of that science). A lot of gay men will clutch their pearls and pucker their face up like they've just eaten a lemon at the mere mention of a vagina, and I think if we are honest with ourselves it is what psychologists call performative disgust.

Performative disgust is when a reaction is expected from someone as part of belonging to a group. When disgust is culturally expected, and the object of that disgust comes up, the reactions of being disgusted are performed. It indicates to the group you're part of the group.

I think a lot of gay men, especially when they first come out of the closet and start to integrate into gay society, pick up on cues about what is required of us. Far too often, disgust at the opposite sex is one such requirement, so we perform it. Perhaps so much we even start believing it. I'm convinced that's what's really driving a lot of the histrionic reactions and simulated dry heaving I see in my community. Now that I know more than 50% of us weren't too repulsed to give it a try, it seems even more likely to me that the revulsion is all for show.

So, is the stereotype true?

I'm convinced by the CDC data. Less than half of gay men have never had any sort of sexual encounter with a female. That Gold Star status doesn't make you more valid as gay. In fact, it doesn't even make you part of the majority.

What's the final verdict?

False.

SCORING YOUR QUIZ: QUESTION #11

In the quiz (page 14), we asked what metal your gay star is made from. Here's how to score your results:

a. Silver: 0 points
b. Gold: 0 points
c. Platinum: 0 points
d. Lead: 0 points

12

You Probably Love Pop Divas

What's the stereotype?

Gay men love and idolize pop divas.

Come on, vogue!

Madonna. Cher. Whitney. Britney. Beyoncé. Kylie. Gays love pop divas so much, we give them mononyms to better revere them. We dance to them at the club, we know every word, and we play their records on repe-pe-pe-pe-peat. From their style to their feminine strength to their meat dresses, gays worship everything about them. But is there any truth to this stereotype? And, if so, why?

Kyle, you love Britney so much! Why do gays love pop divas?

I have to admit, as someone with an unreasonable obsession with Britney Spears, I write this chapter earnestly asking myself this question, wondering where it will lead me. I am the subject about which I'm writing, yet I don't totally understand it myself.

My mind automatically jumps back to the time I couldn't stop listening to the Hanson album with the song *MMMBop*. (I know they're not pop divas, but stick with me.) I loved it. So I, a boy in junior high, told my male junior high friends that I loved Hanson. Little did I know, liking Hanson was "gay." I tried to backpedal, but I was trapped. I had already said that I loved Hanson. I was ridiculed and teased. "That's so gay!" they said to me.

Kyle: *If Britney Spears plays in a forest, will the gays fall over themselves to get there?*

EPISODE 140: BRITNEY SPEARS

In that moment, I learned that I couldn't trust my instincts about what I liked. As a closeted kid, getting called "gay" is one of the most terrifying experiences you can imagine. It's like your secret is right out there in the open, ready to ruin you if you don't deny it hard enough. My biggest fear was getting found out, and liking Hanson almost exposed me. From then on, instead of liking the music I liked, I was resolved to like the music everyone else liked. It was the only way to avoid being found out.

But in private, my love for pop music was still there. As a kid, I watched TRL on MTV alone in my room almost every day. I loved songs like *Oops!... I Did It Again* and *Genie in a Bottle* and *Most Girls*. I knew I couldn't talk about liking them because I knew they were "gay" songs. They were songs only to be enjoyed in the solitary life I led behind the closed doors of my bedroom.

When I finally came out in college, it was a relief to finally be able to like the music I liked, unabashedly. And, you know what? It was more than that, too. It's that I had been forced to hide my appreciation for *this one specific genre* of music. I had been forced to find rock bands that I found tolerable enough to say were my favorite, bands like Puddle of Mudd and System of a Down and Oasis. I had been forced to hide my true self. For the longest time, I couldn't tell anyone I loved Britney Spears (except when I pretended I was into her for her looks). Finally, after coming out, I was able to not just like what I like, but also celebrate what I had been previously ridiculed for: pop music.

In an article on *Attitude*[76] about this subject, Patrick Cash says that, "Pop music, which until that point had made me happy, and made me want to dance, was seen as feminine, and femininity at a boys' [school] was despised." Any interests we have that are stereotypically feminine are looked down upon as boys. Whether it's the *My Little Ponies* I wanted for Christmas or the fact that I wanted to braid hair with the other girls in elementary school, I often got chastised for my more stereotypically feminine interests.

All the while, the women of pop are singing out loud about our hidden interests, not the least of which is boys. These days, there are more and more gay male artists, but when I was a kid, the only place I could go to find someone singing about boys was the women. I could relate to their songs better, albeit secretly. I could express my fascination with boys through their lyrics.

Not to mention that the women of pop would be far more likely to show off hot, shirtless, sweaty men in their videos. I still remember the video for *Most Girls* where P!nk featured jacked men working out, playing instruments, and dancing in the background. Younger me was deeply enamored with this video in the same way I was enamored with Bowflex commercials.

So, you're saying it's just about sex and eye candy?

No, there's more to our interest in pop divas' songs than just boys. In a Master's Thesis,[77] Ramzi Bou Moughalabie interviewed 14 millennial gay men and found that "participants tend to be attracted to [female pop divas'] power and unapologetic nature, as they see in them powerful and independent female figures that they can emulate." In fact, 12 of the 14 men interviewed mentioned "themes of empowerment" as a reason for their interest in pop divas. *Stronger* is now echoing through my head as one of the songs that gave me this feeling of empowerment and, well, strength, telling me I could get through anything.

In a paper about Lady Gaga's fandom,[78] one researcher surveyed 50 fans to understand their interests. In relaying the importance of *Born This Way,* one Gaga fan wrote, "I remember that the day the song was released was a particularly bad day for me. I would venture to say that it gave me the strength I needed to make it." These songs are important to us as more than just songs. Their meaning touches us to our core, sometimes helping us survive, like Gloria Gaynor told us to.

Pop music's upbeat tempo and lyrics help us in our trying times. In fact, in that Master's Thesis, Moughalabie discusses how pop music is a form of escapism. One of the findings from the interviews is that, "growing up gay in a patriarchal society, most participants tend to listen to pop music in order to escape their homophobic realities." For those few moments, watching TRL alone in my room with the doors closed, I could escape the realities of growing up as a closeted gay kid and just enjoy the music (and the shirtless men in the videos).

I think there's something to the fact that women and gays both struggle with full acceptance and equality in society. Both are marginalized communities that want to be treated with respect. While we face different challenges, there's clearly something gays can relate to in women's experience of the world. In an article on Medium,[79] Boby Andika Ruitang states that "divas, for as long as anyone can remember, has [sic] spoken to us about their shared experiences of oppression and how they overcome it, and that's why it's just so damn empowering and why we're so obsessed with it." There's that word again: empowering.

Why is empowerment so important to us?

It's the reason coming out is so important. It's the reason we have to learn to undo our internalized homophobia and shed years of shame.

It's the reason we celebrate Pride every year. We value empowerment because, for so much of our childhood, we feel the opposite. I felt lonely and embarrassed by who I was growing up, so I celebrate anything that helps me find my joy.

In the Medium article, Ruitang also says that, "Their songs channels [sic] their pain, their sufferings, their vulnerabilities, and also their strength to rise up and face the odds." I think gay culture celebrates anyone who overcomes because we want to live in a world where we, too, can overcome.

In many ways, gay culture is infused with pop music, making them indisputably intertwined. Go to a gay club, and you're almost guaranteed to hear the latest from Taylor Swift or Rihanna or Ariana Grande or Dua Lipa. When Kylie or Beyoncé drop a new album, it's the conversation piece for weeks. In the biggest hyperbole I've ever read, Ruitang says, "Put on a Lady GaGa or Christina Aguilera song and I can assure you that 99% of gay men would know the lyrics without missing a beat." OK, so 99% is extreme. But there's something to the idea that we're expected to know all the latest hits and when to clap during *Black Lady.*

Drag queens also build up these pop divas as icons through their acts. Queens, like many gay men, are inspired by the fabulous outfits and glamor of female artists (and, perhaps, vice versa). They lip sync for their lives to pop songs. They dance and earn their tips to them. Drag queens are a source of culture in the gay community, and they, along with the pop music they use in their acts, bring us entertainment, joy, and validation.

OK, so gay men love pop divas, and the verdict is "true," right?

Now let's take a step back. So far, through reading articles and poring through research papers and reflecting on my own experiences, I know there's a strong connection within the gay community and pop divas. There's something to this stereotype. But the thing about stereotypes is that they can sometimes become overblown. So rather than looking at whether *some* gay men love pop divas, I still wanted to know if *all* (or even *most*) gay men love pop divas.

The most tangible data I could find was from an article on Out in Jersey,[80] citing data from Luminate, which is credited as "the data company that powers the Billboard charts." The article states, "LGBTQ listeners are notably more interested in pop and Top 40 music than their non-LGBTQ counterparts," indicating that 34% of LGBTQ respondents listen to pop on a weekly basis. It seems that the data supports the fact that we love our pop music more than the average straight person.

However, that same article also says, "46% of LGBTQ respondents [say] they listen to rock music on a weekly basis." Surprisingly, at least according to this article, rock is more popular among LGBTQ people than even pop. This aligns with the overall trend of music genre popularity in the US. Even if we over-index for our interest in pop music, there are still more rock-lovers than pop-lovers.

It should go without saying that gay people listen to all types of music. I have gay friends that exclusively go to punk shows. Sexuality doesn't equate to musical preference, no matter how much we write about or study it.

When I searched for articles and research studies on the topic of pop, I found link after link to pages asking a similar question: "Why do gay men love pop divas?" I've quoted some of them in this very chapter. On the other hand, when I searched for "why do gay men love rock music," the very first site I got was from Quora with the question, "Why is rock music not more popular with gay men?" There are more articles, of course, some of which detail how rock was created by gay Black men. The interest in other music genres is there, but it may not be as discussed as pop music is.

On the other hand, for some gay men, music just isn't an

YOU PROBABLY LOVE POP DIVAS

important part of their life. One paper[81] interviewed seven gay men to find out if and how music was important to their coming out process. For some of them, music was a companion, and even a catalyst, for their coming out process. They also note, however, that "not all of the interviewees referred to music as a central factor." One of the interviewees mentioned that other forms of media, like TV, movies, and books, helped him during the coming out process. We don't *all* have the same affinity for music.

Plus, there are plenty of straight people that love pop music, too. Straight people aren't immune to its catchy beats. Pop music is called pop because it's popular, which means lots of people enjoy it. Hell, my (straight) brother has professed his love of Kelly Clarkson. I wonder if part of the reason we associate pop music so strongly with gay men (and not straight men) is because it's more socially acceptable for us to openly enjoy it. How many straight men have to hide their interest in pop music for fear of those accusations that they might be gay, just like I did as a kid?

Mike: *When I see my fellow gay men in the universe, any time she's [Beyoncé's] on TV, they're like my dad when we're at the mall and the Mariners game is on; they lose their shit. "Fucking shut up! Beyoncé is on!" Everybody freaks the fuck out, jizzes rainbows, and I just... I don't understand."*

Kyle: *That part's a little bit different than your dad.*

EPISODE 117: BEYONCÉ

So, why is pop music still so strongly associated with the gay community?

Maybe there's a sense of belonging that's built purely through our interest in pop music. That Master's Thesis found that, "Being a fan of a female pop star is sometimes maybe less about the artist, but maybe more about the culture, because it also has this type of communal bonding experience." Similarly, that paper on Lady Gaga fans said, "a crucial aspect of music participation is that it provides individuals with a significant sense of belonging and group membership." I find so much joy in blasting a pop song on the radio in Mike's Jeep, both of us singing at the top of our lungs. Or putting on the latest Kim Petras song at a party and seeing other gay men stop to enjoy it. Or when a pop diva's latest single comes on at the club and everyone rushes to the dance floor. It can make us feel a sense of togetherness, bonding over what used to be nothing but a hidden interest we buried deep down when we were closeted kids. Something we thought we'd never be able to share with anyone, much less a crowd of other people.

I think, as LGBTQ+ rights continue to advance, we'll start to see a shift in who we idolize. We revere our female pop singers because of our shared interest in men, their ability to energize and empower us, and the sense of belonging we found from them. However, as there are more out artists, it will mean a bigger variety of people for us to look up to. We'll have more out gay male pop stars. We'll have more out musicians in every genre. We'll have a bigger variety of people to idolize, not just the straight women.

I also think we'll see a change in the expectations of pop divas. Pop divas are now expected to advocate for the community in order to maintain their gay icon status. One paper,[82] appropriately called "What has she actually *done??!*", analyzed the blog comments of two gay-focused websites and found that "many readers [...] demand that divas engage in gay-rights activism to earn their adoration." We expect more than just their music to earn our loyalty.

In fact, we've already started to see that shift in activism. People like Madonna paved the way with her support of people with AIDS back in the 80s. As just one example, in 1989, she released an album that included a handout called "The Facts about AIDS" that expressed support for those with AIDS, "regardless of their sexual orientation," which, among her many other contributions, has helped her earn the strong, lasting loyalty of gay men.

These days, we're seeing more and more pushes towards activism. Lady Gaga, who is bisexual, started the Born This Way Foundation in 2012 to support the mental health of young people, with LGBTQ+ people often being a focus. Miley Cyrus, who is pansexual, started The Happy Hippie Foundation in 2015 that focuses on homelessness among vulnerable youth, particularly LGBTQ+ youth. Not only are we getting increased visibility from LGBTQ+ pop singers themselves, but we're also seeing increased investment in the LGBTQ+ community through their words of support and direct financial donations. We support them, so we expect them to support us.

The face of pop music will continue to grow and evolve, but I think our community will always have a soft spot for our pop divas. I know bubblegum pop makes up just about all my top music on Spotify. While I do enjoy it for the simple, upbeat joy it brings me, I've learned that, like a good dicking, it goes deeper. I love being able to listen to the music I was made to feel bad about growing up. I love the escapism it provides, especially when I'm having a rough mental health day (and LGBTQ+ people are more likely to struggle with mental health issues; see Chapter 1). I love the memories of singing and dancing to pop singles on the dance floor of the gay bar. I love pop, and clearly, I'm not the only one.

So, is the stereotype true?

Based on not only my personal interest and experience, but also the articles and research studies, it seems there's something to this stereotype. Pop divas are held in high esteem by enough of us that there's a strong association between female pop music and gay men. However, the only tangible data I was able to find shows that rock is more popular among LGBTQ+ people than pop, proving LGBTQ+ people aren't a monolith. We listen to other genres beyond just pop. We come in all shapes and sizes, as do our music interests. We do over-index in our appreciation of pop music, but our interest in pop music doesn't define the entire community.

What's the final verdict?

Somewhat true.

SCORING YOUR QUIZ: QUESTION #12

In the quiz (page 14), we asked which concert you would choose first. Here's how to score your results:

- **a.** Cher opening for Madonna: 2 gay points
- **b.** Maroon 5 opening for Usher: 1 gay point
- **c.** Metallica opening for Bruce Springsteen: 0 gay points
- **d.** Country: -1 gay point

13

You Probably Love Musicals

What's the stereotype?

Any man interested in musical theater is gay.

Gays love Patti LuPone, but who the fuck is she?!

Be careful. That's a question that will elicit a gay gasp in the right room. Musical theater nerds are legion in the gay community. Like any flavor of nerd, the Broadway gays are passionate, full of endless trivia, and more than willing to pass judgment on your lack of knowledge. Expect an exasperated, "Ohmigod what?!? The original Eva Peron in Evita? Rose from the 2008 revival of Gypsy? COME ON NOW!!" It seems so common to run into theater queens in gay circles it has become a staple stereotype.

Mike likes to sing. Does he love musicals?

I am not a theater queen, but I want to be. Lots of gay bars do "musical sing-along" nights, where herds of dudes gleefully sing songs from musical theater, and oddly sometimes Disney tunes, at the top of their lungs. I love going; the energy is infectious. When I manage to make it to one, I don't know all of the songs, but I love to belt out the ones I do know. There's a deep sense of solidarity that all of us in the room, napkins held high in the air for that one special moment from Evita, are doing something super-duper gay together.

Kyle: *Is it Evita that you get out a tissue or something and wave it around?*

Mike: *So much Kleenex wasted.*

Kyle: *I do enjoy musicals, but obviously not to the extent to which a gay man is supposed to, and I feel looked down upon for that.*

EPISODE 209: MUSICALS

It's also nice to know that I will forever know the number of minutes in a year, and if you just sang the answer out loud or heard it in your head, we should be friends.

Musical theater has become ingrained in our collective consciousness as a leading indicator of homosexuality. When I finally came out at 30, one of my fraternity brothers told me, "I guess I sort of already knew you were gay; you never banged any of the chicks that loved hanging in your room while you played guitar and sang, and you *did* know all the words to RENT." I'm not sure what it is about my fraternity brothers and RENT, but that particular musical pops up in my history over and over again.

When I first moved into the Sigma Phi Epsilon house at Eastern Washington University during spring break of my sophomore year in 1998...

Wait, you were a frat guy?

Don't interrupt. Yes, I was a frat guy. No, it wasn't as hot as it sounds since I was mostly terrified. Anyway, my roommate and I discovered our mutual love for the musical RENT. I'd gotten the original cast recording as a gift, for Christmas, I believe, and we basically played it on repeat nonstop. We even started singing it to each other. "You want to be Angel or Collins?" he'd ask. "Collins," I'd say, "the Angel part is a bit high for me." We literally never discussed that the song *I'll Cover You* was about the deepening connection between two gay men.

I remember being terrified that doing something so quintessentially gay would ruin my credibility as a straight frat bro. I was 19, and although I was aware that I was into dudes, I was damned determined to stay in the closet. But this particular roommate had a reputation as a sensitive ladies' man, and even won the "Mister Eastern" pageant no less. Combine that with frat life, homoeroticism of that institution notwithstanding, and at least in our community at that time his straightness was beyond reproach... even if he was singing gay love songs with another dude at the top of his lungs. His shield of hetero energy was enough for both of us to hide behind.

Looking back on it, it's a little odd that we didn't raise more eyebrows. I guess his being a "lady killer" and a borderline local celebrity representing the masculine ideal on campus were what made it OK. Unlike other contexts where there's a presumption of straightness, it's always felt like if you're a man that's into musicals you're gay until proven straight. Enough so that to suggest otherwise is, well, a joke. Neil Patrick Harris hosted the Tony Awards in 2011, and the opening number was titled "It's Not Just for Gays Anymore." If you've not heard it yet you should YouTube it; it's hilarious. In fact, put the book down and go do that. I'll be right here when you get back. *patiently whistles La Vie Boheme*[83]

OK, I've watched it! I'm back.

You're back! Hilarious, right? My favorite part, besides NPH hitting on Angela Lansbury, was the lyric toward the end: "So, people from red states, and people from blue / A big Broadway rainbow is waiting for you / Come in and be inspired / There's no sodomy required!"

Anyway, either my roommate never got the memo that we were being super gay or he was just secure enough in his sexuality to not care. For the record, although he was (and still is) incredibly handsome and charming, I was never into him "that way." Just not my type. Which is all the same since he's married with kids now and seems genuinely straight... although married with kids isn't a slam dunk either. I have another story about RENT and a fraternity brother that illustrates that point.

After graduating from college I worked for the fraternity in the Midwest. One day I carpooled from Chicago to Illinois State for a workshop. Driving that day was another fraternity brother, who at the time was a married man with a child on the way. On the 2 hour ride home that night we sang the RENT soundtrack. Cover to cover. We both knew *every single word*.

We reconnected over 10 years later when he came out. We've laughed and laughed about that day, "just two straight frat bros being super straight singing RENT in the car" and how we're both big ole homos now.

I had yet another fraternity brother that bought a one-way ticket to Broadway in 1999 with dreams of making it big. I remember giving him notes on his audition piece, which was *One Song Glory* from, you guessed it, RENT. Although he took the same path as I did and was married to a lady for a while, he turned out bisexual. Another one bites the dick, I guess.

Four fraternity brothers, including me, and all of us RENT heads. Only one turned out totally straight. Maybe the stigma of gayness that musical theater has is well earned after all. Regardless of where that stigma came from it has had a measurable impact on the business. How to market to straight guys is considered one of the holy grails of the big business of Broadway. In fact, from shows about superheroes to baseball to boxing, a lot of flops over the years have been bets on shows that would get hetero dudes to show up. They did not show up.

According to the New York Times, in 2014 only 32% of the typical Broadway audience was male.[84] So herein lies another example of a phenomenon we see over and over again in this book: if something appeals to women, eventually it's associated with gays. Gays flock to something gay because, well, it's gay. Once the gays are involved, straight men run for the hills and it becomes even gayer. The same NYT article points out that in 1980 the typical audience was 42% men. It still skewed female, but it wasn't nearly as lopsided. And it's entirely possible those 42% aren't exactly there voluntarily. It might be that straight guys don't go to Hamilton; they get dragged there by their wives and girlfriends.

That's front-of-house, though. What about on stage?

Theater is often considered a safe haven for the queer kids. Hell, I think every person I know from high school that turned out gay was on the Drama team. Melissa Gimble on Schmigadoon (played by Cecily Strong) repeated a pretty common saying that attempts to explain musicals. "When you're too emotional to talk, you sing. When you're too emotional to sing, you dance."[85] Well, growing up gay is traumatic. There's a lot of reasons to sing and dance for queer kids. We are attracted to the chance to be someone else for a while in a world that doesn't want us to be who we are.

If you're under the impression that all actors are gay, you'd be wrong, of course. All the gays are hairdressers and flight attendants. I'm kidding, not all actors are gay (see Chapter 10), but it is definitely lopsided. According to Zippia, a site I cannot vouch for, 19% of actors and actresses are LGBTQ+, about double what we'd expect.[86] That might be because while watching a Broadway show might be for chicks, acting is apparently for dudes. 67.55% of actors are men, so maybe the "that's for women and gays" effect hasn't taken hold. It also might just be a question of supply and demand; there are FAR more roles written for men.

But Broadway is only as gay as the people in charge let it be, and the back-of-house, the business of Broadway, is hetero as hell. There is a pink glass ceiling in the industry. It's hard to get exact statistics, but looking at Executive Producer as a title (across all kinds of media), again according to Zippia, they are very much white (65%) hetero (85%) men (65%). It turns out that, at least racially, Broadway itself is far worse than that. According to the Asian American Performers Action Coalition (AAPAC), 93.8% of Broadway Directors are white. 93.6% of Broadway Producers are white. 92.6% of Broadway Designers are white. 100% of Broadway General Managers are white.[87, 88] My guess is that the other two numbers, those that are straight and those that are men, are also pretty damning when we focus on musical theater.

Not that all straight men are bad, just common and with disproportionate power. Many are even good allies. When I was in New York City to do a live show of our podcast, *Gayish,* I had dinner and drinks with that RENT-singing fraternity roommate from all those years ago. We talked a lot about our musical escapades and reminisced about frat life in the 90s. It was the first one-on-one time we'd had in over 20 years. It was great to see him, and something he said that night sticks with me. Talking about the fact we sang gay love songs from musicals to each other, he said, "I don't think anybody really cared. Our room was for music, and everyone was fine with that even if it was RENT." He also told me, "You know, I think if you'd come out (of the closet) when we were undergrads everyone would have been fine with that too."

He seemed to be saying that yeah, musicals are pretty darn gay. He knew it back then, and it's still true now. And yeah, the frat brothers knew that, too. But that, at least to him, looking back through the lens of our shared history, everyone around us was a little more OK with gay stuff than I realized. I'm grateful to him and his hetero shield, and that our room was indeed always filled with song. I'm also grateful he always paid the RENT on time.

So, is the stereotype true?

A lot of stereotypes have a grain of truth in them, and this is one of them. The men in and around musical theater, both in the audience and on stage, tend to be gayer than the general population. There are still plenty of straight men to be found in these spaces, especially on the business side, but the overrepresentation of gay men both on and off stage makes it clear something gay is going on here.

What's the final verdict?

Mostly true.

SCORING YOUR QUIZ: QUESTION #13

In the quiz (page 14), we asked who starred as Fanny Brice in Funny Girl. Here's how to score your results:

- **a.** Barbra Streisand: 2 gay points
- **b.** Lea Michele: 1 gay point
- **c.** Janeane Garofalo: 0 gay points
- **d.** Isn't Fanny the British word for vagina?: -1 gay point

14
You Probably Have Good Gaydar

What's the stereotype?

People have an intuitive ability to tell whether someone else is gay based on things like appearance, mannerisms, and dress (i.e. gaydar).

It comes naturally to gay people, right?

Can you tell someone is gay just by looking at them? What if they have bleach blond hair? What if they're well dressed? What if they stand with their hand on their hip? What if you can hear them speak, and you can detect a hint of a lisp in their voice? What if you get a gut feeling that just screams in your head, "they're totally gay!" Some people, especially gay men, believe they can tell. That's the crux of gaydar. The idea that, based on things like appearance, mannerisms, and dress, they can just *tell* if someone is gay or not.

Kyle, can you break down the gayta?

Gaydar, a portmanteau of "gay" and "radar," first came up during the 80s or 90s, and it seemed to pop up everywhere. The word "gaydar" appeared in shows like *Will & Grace, Seinfeld, Futurama,* and *Queer Eye for the Straight Guy.* Gaydar.com was a gay dating website that started in 1999. "Gaydar" was even the name of a 2002 short film that boasts Charles Nelson Reilly's last movie appearance. It seems like we've been talking about, and potentially believing in, the concept of gaydar for decades, maybe longer. Many of my friends have nudged me and whispered, "Hey, is he gay?" as they point to someone I've never met. Oftentimes, I'd take a guess. But is it really possible?

Now, a disclaimer: if someone explicitly tells you their sexual orientation or their gender, believe them. It sucks to come out as gay just to be told "you just haven't met the right girl." On the flip side, I'm sure it sucks to have to constantly tell people you're straight, even though you have a nice shoe collection. If someone hasn't told you explicitly, don't make assumptions. Use gender neutral language to describe them, and don't presume who they might be interested in sexually, or that they have any sexual interest at all.

Some researchers even caution against using the word "gaydar" at all. Calling it gaydar may make it seem fun or lighthearted, like a game. Dr. William Cox wrote[89] in CNN that, according to one of his studies, when people were told that gaydar is real, they tended to stereotype more. Stereotyping fuels prejudice, and prejudice against a group of people is bad. Gaydar really is serious business.

While all of that is important to keep in mind, that's not what this chapter is about; we're not talking about social etiquette. It's about whether there's any grain of truth to the idea of gaydar, with all the gravity that the idea would bring.

So, is there any grain of truth to it?

Turns out, there is. In the paper "Perceptions of Sexual Orientation From Minimal Cues,"[90] prominent gaydar researcher Dr. Nicholas

Rule reviews existing academic studies, many of them his own. Essentially, it's a state of the union on gaydar research as of 2017, which is when the paper came out in the journal *Archives of Sexual Behavior*. He includes research on various cues that we use to (try to) intuit sexual orientation, including adornment, acoustics, actions, appearance, automatic processing, and facial features. Damn, couldn't get that last one to alliterate. Each one was supported by multiple different studies, but I want to share my favorites:

- *Adornment:* This includes the way we dress, our hair, and our style. The studies seem to say that gays and lesbians are more likely than their straight counterparts to break the gender stereotypes of appearance. My favorite example was a study that said women would often change their appearance after coming out, including cutting their hair short.
- *Acoustics:* There is a distinct way gay people speak, such as the infamous lisp. Surprisingly, this section was the least convincing to me, but there was one study that confirmed gay and straight people have different ways of speaking, although "pinning down the precise parameters that account for these differences has proved elusive."
- *Actions:* Gay people move their body differently than straight people. One study showed that gay men and straight women tend to sway their hips more, while straight men and lesbians tend to swagger their shoulders. In another study, they reviewed home footage of gay and straight children, and children that grew up to be gay moved in what was deemed "sex-atypical" ways, i.e. ways that broke the stereotypes of their gender.
- *Appearance:* This encompasses the body of the person in question. I was surprised to learn that studies found that straight

men and lesbians were taller than gay men and straight women, respectively, and they have shorter limbs. (Given I'm 6'3", this one doesn't quite work for me.)

- *Automatic processing:* This is the idea that our gaydar may be happening immediately, like a snap judgment. In one study, researchers showed pictures of straight and gay men's faces for participants to guess their sexual orientation. Participants that were asked to trust their gut were more accurate than participants that were asked to deliberate for some time before responding. In another study, after seeing a gay or straight man's face, participants were asked to play a word formulation game. When shown a gay face, they formed gay-stereotyped words (e.g. rainbow) faster, and when shown a straight face, they formed straight-stereotyped words (e.g. football) faster.

- *Facial features:* Individual parts of our faces can reveal a lot of information about who we are. Studies found that, when isolating various parts of the face, including just eyes, just mouths, or just hairstyle, people could still determine, better than chance, if they were gay. There are also studies that try to determine if and how our faces are different, and one study found that straight men had more symmetrical faces than gay men.

There seemed to be a dearth of studies that indicated there are various physical ways we differ from straight people, some discernible with a tape measurer, but most measured by participants guessing whether they thought someone was gay based on their movement, eyes, voice, etc. They were trying to measure gaydar in a lab. In these cases, I would often see the line "better than chance." Chance would suggest participants have a 50-50 shot at guessing whether someone was gay or straight, like flipping a coin. However, participants could often determine if someone was gay "better than chance."

So, how much "better than chance" are we at guessing sexual orientation?

You're asking how accurate is gaydar? In this paper, Rule offers that the accuracy in determining if someone gay is above 60%, depending on which measure we're referring to. 60% > 50%, therefore gaydar is real. Some criticize these studies by saying you can't take these lab-designed experiments and apply them to the real world because of the obvious: the real world isn't a lab. I'd argue that each one of these are being taken in isolation, so if someone had the benefit of a holistic view of a person, the entirety of their actions and face and body and dress and hair and voice, that may mean we could be more accurate than even the 60%. Then again, I don't have "Dr." in front of my name.

Another criticism of gaydar is in the name. It's only focused on gay. What about the variety of other sexual identities that someone can be, aside from just gay or straight? I saw some studies use a modified Kinsey scale. In one study, they directly addressed this with the participants of the study, the ones that were making the judgment. People tended to view gay and bisexual similarly, which led the researchers to determine people were really deciding whether someone is straight or not straight. So, gaydar might be more accurately called "non-straight-dar," but that doesn't quite roll off the tongue. In another study, participants could "reliably" determine if someone was gay or straight, but not bisexual. Maybe there's no bi-dar after all? I think gay stereotypes are ingrained into society, whereas bi stereotypes are less defined and pervasive, making them harder to spot in studies.

Also, Dr. William Cox (yup, the same one from the CNN article) and his colleagues tried to replicate one of Rule's studies by using people's pictures from dating sites and asking if people could tell if they were gay or straight. They first found that gay and lesbian pictures were of higher quality, which they believe could explain some of the outcomes. Maybe we can tell if someone is gay because gay people take better pictures. When they excluded those with higher quality, they couldn't replicate Rule's results. Instead, they found that people were no better than chance at telling someone's orientation, meaning gaydar wasn't real. Rule countered this by saying that some studies use photos that were taken in a lab to ensure they were standardized. It also ignores all of the evidence that doesn't rely on photographs, such as the height difference between gay men and straight men.

Yet another criticism is that studies often use 50-50 as the comparison: people are either gay or straight. However, in the real world, there is a much smaller percentage of gay men than that, let's say 5–10%. So, even if you're 60% accurate, if you try to apply the lab learnings to the real world, that means there are a lot of straight men you're going to mistake for being gay. I tend to ignore this criticism as I think we as humans, and especially as gay men, understand that, in the real world, gay men are far less prevalent than straight men, and we use that to inform our gaydar. In other words, he's probably straight until we find a clue or a gut feeling that says otherwise.

But wait! There are even more complexities. Some studies show that *who* is making the guess is important, too. In Rule's paper, there is an example of a study that says people who are anti-gay do worse than those more familiar with gay men. To directly answer the question of whether gay men have better gaydar than others, the paper said, "sexual minorities may show better accuracy in judging others' sexual orientation from faces, but show only a small and inconsistent advantage for judgments based on other channels (e.g., speech, movement), including appearance beyond the face." So, your personal gaydar may be better or worse than others because of a variety of factors, some of which you may have no control over.

In addition, the internal qualities of the person being judged matter. For example, one study showed that the faces of gay men with greater internalized homophobia were harder to categorize than those that were more comfortable with their gayness. Maybe self-hatred makes you more likely to try to disguise your gayness.

Many other papers exist with far more intelligent and scientific criticism than I could possibly relay. There's "The science of stereotyping: Challenging the validity of 'gaydar'" by Devin Lowe. There's "Gaydar and the fallacy of objective measurement" by Gelman, Mattson, and Simpson. There's "Inferences About Sexual Orientation: The Roles of Stereotypes, Faces, and The Gaydar Myth" by Cox (the same one from CNN), Devine, Bischmann, and Hyde. It seems that, because some studies picked up media attention, there was a flurry of papers that came out trying to counter the claims made by both the media and the research itself. So, at best, all I can say is that science has yet to agree on whether gaydar is real.

Mike: *The [government of the] country of Kuwait was researching in the early 2010s a way to detect gay people so that they would be prevented from entering the country.*

Kyle: *Oh, shit. I heard about this on Kuwait, Kuwait, Don't Tell Me.*

EPISODE 228: GAYDAR

OK, so it's complicated. What do YOU think, Kyle?

Even with all the criticisms in mind, I believe that there's something to gaydar. There are clearly some measurable differences between gay and straight people. I keep coming back to the phrase "sex-atypical." I think one of the things that may contribute to that 60% number is that gay people have already broken one social norm. No matter the progress we've made, straightness is still the default assumption. Statistically, it should be. So, once we've broken out of default in one area of our life, we have more leeway to break out of the defaults in other areas. Lesbians may cut their hair after they come out. Gay men may let their hips sway or let their lisps out. Maybe we do some of that on purpose to try to signal to others that we're gay. Maybe it happens naturally because we're no longer trying to mask the qualities that we were worried would out us. Regardless, I can accept that *some of us* are more likely to break societal norms of gender expectations. Even ignoring things like the facial symmetry and the shorter limbs, breaking the norms might be more common for gay people. However, it's not the rule. Gay people don't have to break the norm, even after they come out. Straight people can break gender norms, too. But if we assume it's more likely for gay people than straight, I could see where we'd end up with a number around 60%.

After all that, what do we do with that information?

It's important to remember that gaydar is, by definition, stereotyping. It's taking broad generalizations about a group of people and applying it to individuals. While researchers had the luxury of testing their theory over many participants, we are individuals trying to use gaydar on another individual. Even if you believe in the 60% accuracy number, that's averaged over a lot of people, and doesn't apply to each and every person. Gaydar isn't really something you can use in the real world with confidence.

While the research is interesting, hopefully it doesn't change your behavior at all, at least not outwardly. Like I mentioned at the beginning, you shouldn't make assumptions about anyone's sexual orientation and, if they tell you, you should believe it. You can have your suspicions or your personal belief that your gaydar is always right, but you shouldn't go around outwardly making assumptions about individuals. Even if it's a fun little game you play by yourself, usually you should just keep it to yourself.

So, is the stereotype true?

Research into gaydar has shown that, on average, we have a better-than-chance shot at telling if someone is gay. However, even without considering all the academic papers that have challenged this idea, 60% effective still isn't very effective in the real world. On an individual basis, we don't have a highly accurate innate ability to sense if someone else is gay. There is no real-world gaydar.

What's the final verdict?

Mostly false.

SCORING YOUR QUIZ: QUESTION #14

In the quiz (page 14), we asked if you were surprised when Anderson Cooper came out. Here's how to score your results:

a. Yes, he seemed so butch!: 0 gay points (because did he really, though?)
b. No, I knew the whole time: 0 gay points (just because you were right about one celebrity doesn't make gaydar real)
c. What? He's gay?!?: -1 gay point (because where have you been?)

15

You're Probably a Slut

What's the stereotype?

Gays are incredibly sexually promiscuous and have hundreds, if not thousands of different sexual partners over their lifetime.

How many sexual partners are we talking?

Have you fucked over 15 people? 100? 500? 1000? With three zeroes? Whatever your number, if you're a gay man the expectation seems to be that it's higher than any other category of human. Given the hypersexual portrayal of gay men in the media, we seem to just accept that as the truth.

Hey, Mike, are gay dudes sluts?

Honestly, y'all, this one makes me nervous. Like, the question "are gay dudes sluts" makes me do a full body :grimace: emoji. Some of that is just shame placed on me by a puritanical society that hates sex in general and gay sex in particular. I've tried really hard my whole gay career to shake that shame, but I know that is a lifetime process. Internalized homophobia is a real bitch. But, in essence, some part of me can't help but feel if gay dudes really are measurably more slutty, it means the smug judgment of all those uppity (let's face it, probably religious) sodomy-hating folks is grounded in some level of truth that makes me super uncomfortable. If their problem is that we fuck too much, we deserve their ire.

But there's also the shame that I feel in being deficient as a gay man. I just rarely enjoy casual anonymous transactional sex. Whether it's true or not, gay men are supposed to be nonstop crazy sex machines, and I'm... just not. I've long looked around the gay community, observing the sex lives of my peers (or at least heard their stories), felt like I was banging less than everyone else, and wondered what it says about me. When I have pursued a life of promiscuity, especially right after I came out and thought that was what was expected of me, my attempts at such a life have never been very enjoyable to me.

The thing is, I have a trauma response to sex a lot of the time, and many a sexual tryst has ended with me just dissociating while I pray he gets off quickly so I can exit the situation. I don't know where that trauma response comes from. I have no history of sexual abuse or trauma. But it is very real and extremely uncomfortable for me when it happens. Historically it happens to me a lot, over half the time. Maybe 80%, honestly.

I have learned that I can load the dice (heh... load) and reduce the chance that I'll have that trauma response. That chance is never zero, but one thing dramatically improves the chance I'm going to have fun and feel satisfied: comfort. I can't get comfortable when there's stranger danger.

The only way for me to be comfortable is to have a modicum of trust with that person. The only way for me to build that trust is to have some sort of connection. The only way for me to build that connection is a face to face conversation, maybe over a cocktail or at a bar, but definitely more than just on Grindr or eye contact at a gloryhole. I don't have to be in love. I just have to connect and know that they are a human being and that they know that I'm a human being, and that we're invested in each other's pleasure and not merely our own. If I feel in the slightest like I'm being used, the chances I'll be triggered are very, very, very high.

It's taken me a long time to accept that I'm wired this way, and a lot of therapy to realize that it doesn't make me less of a man or homosexually deficient. For the longest time, I struggled with the label demisexual to describe myself. At first glance it sort of seems to apply. Good ole Wikipedia says: "A demisexual person can only experience secondary sexual attraction—the type of attraction that occurs after the development of an emotional bond."[91]

Isn't that what you're describing for yourself?

No, or at least I'd argue it isn't. The sentence directly before that on Wikipedia says "Demisexuality is a sexual orientation in which an individual does not experience primary sexual attraction—the type of attraction that is based on immediately observable characteristics such as appearance or smell and is experienced immediately after a first encounter." That's what makes the label not feel right for me... I'm very much deeply, animalistically, viscerally sexually attracted all the time. Hot men turn me on, well before we've even spoken a word to each other. It's not about desire for me, but ability. Demisexuality, at least according to Wikipedia, means a lack of desire before the connection.

Being like this has led me to the belief that I'm a prude. I keep it in my pants more than my fellow gays. My guess is that my lifetime count of sexual partners is low compared to my peers. If this stereotype of gay men as category 5 sexual hurricanes is correct, but I'm a tropical storm at best, I'm therefore somehow flawed or a failure.

So... get to the point, Mike. Are gay dudes sluts or not?

Well, first of all, "sluts" is such a loaded word. It is such puritanical bullshit. The Catholic Church has been saying for centuries now that any pleasure from sex, even inside a marriage, is dirty and sinful. Back in the 4th century, a long ass time ago, St. Augustine believed any sexual pleasure was the result of original sin and that it involved a loss of rational control. (He might be right about the rational control part, if you've ever witnessed the behavior of gay bar patrons at last call.) St. Augustine also seems... kinda gay? He once wrote, "I do not see what sort of help woman was created to provide man with, if one excludes procreation. If woman is not given to man for help in bearing children, for what help could she be? [...] How much more pleasure is it for life and conversation when two [dude] friends live together than when a man and a woman cohabitate?"[92] Basically he thinks all women are good for is birthing children, and he thinks nonstop dude time would be fantastic if we didn't need babies. At any rate, St. Augustine is one of the Eight Doctors of the (Catholic) Church, and he's just one example of how we've been looking down on people for enjoying sex for well over 1600 years. Longer, really; the Old Testament of the Bible could be considered more of the same.

As a gay recovering Catholic, though, I give zero shits what the church thinks anymore, especially about my naughty bits. But their impact on society's views on sex, including my own, is undeniable. The judgment and shame run deep.

You're stalling... Tell me where the sluts are.

Fair. I'll attempt to move past the stigma surrounding the word "slut" and the implication it's not OK to enjoy sex. Let's instead try to narrow down who counts as a slut. That exercise brings up a whole bunch of interesting questions. How many sexual partners is "a lot"? What counts as "sex" for determining whether someone counts as a sexual partner? Do gay men have more sexual partners than straight men? Do men have more sexual partners than women? And, perhaps most importantly, if gay men really do have way more sexual partners than every other category of human, why? And what does it mean?

A dude named Dr. Christopher Badcock, and no I'm not making his last name up, claimed in a blog post from 2017 on Psychology Today titled "It's the Mode for Men to Have More Sex Partners" that "one study in San Francisco found that nearly 50% of gay men had more than 500 partners."[93] Holy Badcock, Batman! I don't know what I expected "a lot" to be, but 500 definitely feels like it. He also doesn't provide a link to that study, and I'll be damned if I can find out exactly where those numbers came from. Bad Badcock.

> **Mike:** *Does your milkshake bring* all *the boys to the yard?*
>
> **Kyle:** *My yard is only so big, you know? There's a significant number it brings to the yard, but we have to really phase in turns, there's a waiting list, there's a fast pass.*
>
> **Mike:** *You have one of those "Please Take a Ticket" and "Now Serving 12" signs?*
>
> **Kyle:** *Sometimes it serves 12, 13, and 14.*
>
> **EPISODE 115: FASHION**

It's possible that he's referring to a book called *Homosexualities*, written by Alan Bell and Martin Weinberg in 1978. In it they claimed that 43% of gay men they interviewed in the San Francisco Bay Area had over 500 sexual partners in their lifetime. They also claimed 28% of gay men, over a quarter of us, had over 1000 sexual partners.[94] With three zeroes.

The problem? All of the interviews were conducted at gay

bathhouses and brothels, and approximately 25% of the interviewees were sex workers. No shade to sex work at all; I fully support them and the legitimacy of their work. It seems likely though that if your lifetime body count includes paying customers, it's bound to be quite a bit higher than the average if you're good at your job. That book was groundbreaking in a number of ways, but it was deeply deeply flawed, and nobody takes its numbers seriously anymore except right-wing dickbag fuckface assholes with an axe to grind.

So, maybe it's just a few really really horny gay dudes driving the number?

That is definitely a theory that I have heard before. The last thing you probably want is a math lesson, but that's how I roll, so here we go. Let's say you have a group of five people. I dunno, maybe they're ABBA fans or something. Now, let's say each of those Dancing Queens have been to an ABBA concert 1, 2, 3, 4, and 5 times respectively. The *mean,* also known as average, number of times they've heard Mamma Mia live is three. The *median,* or middle number, is also three. Now imagine those same ABBA fans, but they've gone to see those Swedish legends sing Take a Chance On Me 1, 2, 3, 4, and 1000 times. With three zeroes. The median, that middle number, is still three. The mean, however, is now 202. So if you were to say "ABBA fans have gone to their concerts an average of 202 times" you are technically correct.* That is indeed the average. But one superfan has Waterloo-ed enough times to make that a deeply misleading number in terms of the story it tells. This is known as "positive skew" in the data.

Turns out that there is a positive skew in the numbers for lifetime

---

* A friend of mine at work likes to say "technically correct is the best kind of correct" and it makes me laugh every single time even though I think she is deeply deeply wrong about that.

sex partnerships of gay men. There is a subset of gay men that are, well, going to a lot of ABBA concerts compared to the rest of us. And, of course, by ABBA concerts I mean orgies. In their 1997 study of the sexual profiles of 2583 older homosexuals published in *The Journal of Sex Research,* Paul Van de Ven, et al., found that as many as "15.7 percent [of homosexuals] reported having had more than one thousand lifetime sexual partners."[95] 1000. With three zeroes.

While there is positive skew in that data, however, it doesn't fully explain away what seems to be a clear major difference between gay men and straight men. One study, a sex survey performed in 2003 in Seattle, shows that gay men really are just on another level than any other category of human. While 69% (nice) of straight dudes responded that they'd had fewer than 15 sexual partners in their life, 93% of the gay dudes said they'd had 15 or more.[96] Women, straight and gay alike, were well under the numbers reported by even the straight dudes.

I'm not sure how the study arrived at 15 as the number to watch. I don't know whether they had data that suggested it was the right place to draw a line or just picked it out of a hat. Either way I guess it seems as good a number as any to call a baseline, since it illustrates the point. For most categories of human, 15 partners is the upper end of the scale for body count, and for the vast majority of gay dudes that's just getting started.

So, Mike, are you a slut too?

Well, here's the thing: if 15 is the line, then yes I am. I can proudly say I've officially been a slut since 2008. I don't even have to get creative about what kind of sex counts as sex in order to hit that threshold either. I know this because I have a spreadsheet. Yeah, it's weird. I know it is. But I was hoping that maybe if I kept track of my sex life I'd be able to figure out why it was only fun for me every once in a while. I was working on fixing that whole "not quite a demisexual" thing I talked about earlier in the chapter.

My spreadsheet, as of this writing, is just a little over 200 people. It freaks me out to type that, to be honest. But I do think it's important to talk about what I mean by sex. My personal definition of sex is "*anything* done between two or more people that if done long enough *could* lead to at least one of them having an orgasm." In my personal philosophy, it's important to be inclusive and not just make it about penises and what is stimulating them. I also believe that orgasm isn't required, although I do think the *possibility* of one is needed. Part of my point there is that cuddling by itself isn't sex, but if you and a consenting partner start going at it but fall asleep before you cum it definitely still counts as sex. There are lots of different ways to make people climax, and if what's happening makes that even a possibility, I think it should count as sex. So my spreadsheet includes a wide array of encounters that I count as sex for me but that others might not.

Many people have a tighter (nice) definition for sex. On the other end of the spectrum, they believe sex is specifically anal or vaginal penetration. Some folks even believe the orgasm part isn't optional if it is going to count; someone has to cum. On my deeply weird spreadsheet, I do keep track of whether the encounter included P-in-the-A or P-in-the-V. It's a checkbox, if you must know. But, even by this narrower definition I'm still solidly in slut territory. As of this writing, 37 and counting. More than double the slut barrier, but a far cry from 1000. With three zeroes.

I'll be honest; a small part of me was hoping that, by that stricter definition of sex, I'd come in under 15 so I could hold onto this self-image as a sheltered prude. I didn't want to be called a demisexual, but I'm not sure I'm ready to be called a slut either. One silver lining: maybe I can get rid of this nagging feeling that I'm "deficient as a gay man" after all. My belief that my body count means I'm a prude just isn't backed up by my own data. Just like the demi label, I guess I have some uncomfortable realignment to do between who I think I am, and who I actually am. Thank god I have a good therapist.

So, is the stereotype true?

There is the old adage that a slut is anyone who has had more sex than you have. As a category, gay men by that measure can be called sluts by every other category of human. While 15 appears to be the upper limit of propriety for most of society, 93% of gay men, at least in one study, are beyond that, and some of us by a longshot. Despite my shame about the whole thing, which I'm going to work on, it seems pretty conclusive to me.

What's the final verdict?

True.

SCORING YOUR QUIZ: QUESTION #15

In the quiz (page 14), we asked you your "body count." Here's how to score your results:

a. 0–15: 0 gay points (could go either way, really)
b. Over 15: 2 gay points (because that's pretty gay of you)
c. Over 1000, with 3 zeroes: 5 points

16

You Probably Get Drunk and High

What's the stereotype?

Gays drink and do drugs more than straight people.

Sounds fun to me!

Gays love to party, whether that's during Pride, fetish night at a leather bar, or mimosas with the ladies. We're at the gay bars every weekend, and we go hard. We drink vodka soda like an alcoholic fish swimming in vodka soda. We do coke in the bathroom. We pop pills on the dance floor. We do meth. Gays. Like. To. Party. Or, at least, that's the stereotype.

Hey, Kyle, you seem like you know how to party.

I still remember the first time I went to a gay club. It was like a rite of passage, almost as important as coming out or sucking dick for the first time. It was my sophomore year of college, and I didn't know much about gay culture other than what I learned from Kathy

Griffin stand-up specials on Bravo. I was out, but only recently, so I had no idea how to be gay. I saw other gays around me that were the life of the party. They always had a witty comment. They were social butterflies. That wasn't me. I thought gay clubs were the source of all the fun and joy and sex and gayness that I had been missing out on, and it was time to change that.

I went with one of my best girl friends. Even though she was straight, she was the safety blanket I brought with me into this new world I was anxious to explore. While I was there, I got hit on by an older gentleman who said I had a "Roman-looking face" (read: big nose), got trashed, danced on the dance floor to club remixes of pop songs, and made out with a boy that I probably shouldn't have. So, I think I covered all my bases for a stereotypical first night out.

Since then, gay bars have continued to evolve in what they mean to me. When I first moved to Seattle, I befriended one of the other gays I worked with and plugged myself into his social group. The only time we hung out outside of the office was on Friday or Saturday nights when we went to Purr, the place to see and be seen, to judge and be judged. As I built my own friend group, if we weren't getting drunk at one of their homes, the weekend meant going out to a gay bar and drunkenly dancing the night away. (Side note: if you want to play a fun, ironic drinking game while reading this section, take a drink every time I say drink, drank, or drunk.)

Now that I'm 37, I care less about being at the cool spots. I don't want to spend time dressing up in nice clothes I hate to impress people I don't know. I prefer the chill gay bars where I can sit and have a drink and a conversation. Where I can let my hair down and be my gay self, protected in a sanctuary that doesn't judge me. I've spent a lot of my out life at gay bars.

Turns out, I'm not alone. A 2005 study[97] looked at whether gays do, in fact, spend more time in bars and found that, compared to lesbians, bisexuals, and straights,* "gay men spend significantly more time in bars." And we're not talking small differences. Among the other groups surveyed, anywhere from 10–25% of them go to a bar at least once a month. For gay men, about 55% go to a bar once a month. I guess we don't like watching *RuPaul's Drag Race* at home alone.

One reason we seek the shelter of gay bars is that they have historically been our safe space. Because of societal judgment and homophobic laws, being gay in public often wasn't (and isn't, depending on where you live) an option. Sometimes, it was downright illegal. Gays were considered deviants. So, where would deviants go? The only place that allowed them to be themselves.

But what does that mean for our actual drinking habits?

Broadly speaking, LGBTQ+ people are, in fact, more likely to drink than the straights. There was a 2015 survey by the US Substance Abuse and Mental Health Services Administration (SAMHSA)[98] that claims it's "the first nationally representative, federally collected comprehensive information on substance use and mental health of adults by sexual orientation." How fancy. According to them, 64% of "sexual minorities" (i.e. lesbians, gays, and bisexuals) reported drinking in the past month vs. 56% of straights. So, yes, more of us drink, but it's not as drastic as some people think. Eight percentage points doesn't make us all party monsters.

Also, it's not the gay men with the largest differences in drinking behavior compared to the straights; it's other identities. Several studies I looked at, including the SAMHSA one, indicated that lesbians

....

* Over the course of doing our podcast, we've learned that there's limited research available on even gays and lesbians. Bisexual people are sometimes included as a distinct group, but often forgotten. Trans people are rarely included. Much more work needs to be done in academic research to ensure all LGBTQ+ people are studied, not just gays and lesbians.

and bisexual women drink significantly more than straight women. Most notably, a 2009 study reported that, among gays, lesbians, bisexuals, and straights, "25% of bisexual women reported heavy drinking—the highest rate of any group."[99] (The possible reasons, as explained by another paper, include "increased socialization in bars and more widespread adoption of masculine traits compared with heterosexual women."[100]) Yet another study reviewed existing literature on trans people and alcohol, and it found that, "despite the limitations of current research, there are consistent findings of a high prevalence of hazardous drinking among transgender populations, such as binge drinking in excess of general population estimates."[101] (No explanation of why was offered.) Compare those findings to men, where that SAMHSA survey found that sexual minority men and straight men actually had similar rates of heavy drinking. Many other studies echo a similar finding. So, in short, when it comes to gay men, we may go to bars more than straight men, but a similar number of us drink heavily.

In addition to gay bars being our safe(r) spaces, another, perhaps more important, reason we drink is as a numbing agent. We've mentioned that gay people are more likely to deal with things like depression, anxiety, and other mental health issues as a result of societal mistreatment and homophobia. Alcohol is a very effective solution when you're feeling shitty, but it's a short-term one. One can, in fact, make things much, much harder in the long run.

Speaking of numbing agents, let's get to the drugs. Jumping back to that 2015 SAMHSA survey, it says that gays are three times more likely than straight men to do illicit drugs, such as marijuana, coke, heroin, or meth. And gays aren't alone. Bisexual men, bisexual women, and lesbians are all far more likely than straights to do drugs. Overall, nearly four in ten sexual minorities use drugs. It's important to note that most of that can be accounted for by weed. Putting "weed" in with the "illicit drug" category is technically true, but feels a little misleading. Not only is it legal in some states, but I also think weed is far less harmful than even alcohol, and I'd much rather someone do loads of weed than drink loads of alcohol.

Still, sexual minorities use drugs more than straight people in all nine of the other (non-weed) categories of drugs that the survey measured. For coke, 5.1% of sexual minorities have used it in the past year, which is 2.8 times more than straights. For hallucinogens, it's 5%, which is 3.1 times more than straights. For meth, it's 2.3%, which is 3.8 times more than straights. We do, in fact, use drugs much more than straight people do.

At the same time, we're not talking about a majority of gay people. "More likely to use" doesn't mean "all." Our brains often default to binary thinking. Either gays use drugs or they don't. They're party animals or they're not. But the actual data isn't as black and white. Less than 5% of the gay men surveyed had done coke in the previous year. Less than 4% had done ecstasy. Less than 2% had done LSD. Sure, some people may lie on a survey, so even if the numbers are really double, triple, quadruple what is being reported, we're still talking about a minority of gay men. Not all gays do drugs. Most don't.

So, um... Kyle... do you?

I remember watching the 1999 US version of *Queer as Folk* when I was in my mid-twenties, long after it had aired. I remember Brian popping a pill into Michael's mouth (or was it Michael into Brian's?), and then they danced the night away at Babylon. After watching that scene, I remember thinking that all gays did drugs, and I just wasn't cool enough to know the kinds of club gays that popped pills and danced shirtless in glitter pants every weekend. None of the gay friends I went out with did. Or, at least, they didn't with me. I think growing up feeling insecure about my very identity—about being gay—made me more prone to wanting to fit in. To be just like everyone else. I was in the closet for 19 years, so I was an expert at fitting in with what was expected of me.

Coming out was a huge step forward, but it also didn't fix all my problems. Suddenly, I was trying to fit in with the new expectations people had of me as a gay man. I would make jokes about not understanding football even though I knew all the rules. I grew up in Texas watching it, after all, albeit from the sidelines with the marching band. I would order appletinis at the bar because I didn't know what drinks I liked. People would always assume I was up to date on the latest pop culture gossip, even after I had stopped caring about staying in the loop.

What I'm saying is, coming out doesn't suddenly change who you are. All my fears, insecurities, and doubts were still right there, built up inside of me. Only now, they were painted in rainbow colors. And with all that, the only gay TV show I had seen was rubbing it in my face, that the main characters, the ones that are supposed to represent some universal gay experience, did drugs. So, when I saw someone mention that they did drugs on Grindr, I eagerly accepted their offer to get me high. That was the first time I did meth.

In truth, it wasn't just that I saw drugs on *Queer as Folk*. It wasn't just that I felt insecure. It wasn't just that I was trying to fit in with a part of gay culture I felt I had been missing out on. It was everything. It was depression. It was hating myself. It was a lack of regard for my personal health or safety. But most of all, it was my decision. I'm the one who decided to take that step for the first time. I'll regret that decision for the rest of my life.

I don't want to lie. Doing meth feels amazing. The depression and the hating myself and the insecurity and the fear, it all disappears. My cares just melt away, and I feel good. And horny. In the gay world, it's often done while watching porn and fooling around with one or more guys. Usually, the host will lay out towels on the couch because doing meth makes people, especially me, sweat like crazy.

They'll put porn on one or two screens, on their TV and on their laptop. I'll usually suck dick, even if the other guy can't get hard. Meth makes it hard to get hard. A lot of guys I know would take a Viagra to combat meth dick. I may even get fucked, if a guy can get it up, and I won't really care by who. Anyone. Everyone. It makes me do things (and people) I wouldn't normally do. And it all feels good.

Then, the crash. One guy I did meth with said that, after the first time he did it, he thought he would never be happy again. I've gotten used to the meth crash. Or, I learned to tolerate it as retribution for what I've done. For maybe three or four days after I use meth, I cancel on my friends and miss appointments. My already high level of depression gets even worse. I think about suicide because I don't want to have to keep fighting through all the bullshit I'm dealing with. Coming down from meth is a horrible feeling.

That horrible feeling is why, for a lot of people, they end up using meth again. When you feel like you'll never be happy again, it makes sense that you turn back to the one thing you know can make you feel good. Luckily, that wasn't my experience. After that first time, I didn't do it again for a while, maybe a year. Then, I did it again. And then, maybe a few months later, I did it again. I did meth a few more times, usually spaced out by several months each time. Eventually, I got a boyfriend, and I didn't do meth again for a while. Turns out, being happy in a new relationship is good drug prevention, at least for me.

Part of me wondered what the big deal was. I, like many elementary school kids in the US, was exposed to Drug Abuse Resistance Education classes, also known as D.A.R.E. My takeaway from D.A.R.E. was that if you do a drug once, you'll get addicted. So, when I wasn't immediately itching to do it every day, I thought I was special. That I was just good enough that I could dabble in meth use whenever I wanted and I would be fine. Yes, I felt the horrible crash after using meth, but I could lie or cover up my tracks well enough that no one knew. I thought it was like drinking, that I could do it whenever I wanted and stop whenever I wanted. I could be an occasional meth user. I was fine. Everything was just fine.

When my boyfriend and I broke up, I used meth again, on and off. And I kept using meth on and off. Sometimes it would be a year between uses. Other times it would be months. But I still thought I was fine. That I could manage my meth use, the crash, the urge to use again, all of it. But the older I got, the more meth use just kept popping up. I would run into a hard time, like not having a job, and I'd use it more often. Then I'd pull back. I kept dipping in over and over and over until I realized I was using about once a month consistently. The realization struck me, so I decided I'd try to go without for a while. I failed, and I kept using about once a month. I thought I could stop whenever I wanted, but, as it turns out, I couldn't. Even when I tried to quit for good, I'd end up having a bad day or getting black-out drunk or just needing a temporary release from all the pain I was feeling, and I'd go back to meth. I hate that it's part of my life.

I'm working on self-acceptance in therapy. Hell, I feel like I'm working on it all the time these days. Whatever validation or escape or joy that meth has given me, I'm trying to find from elsewhere. I'm trying not to need a drug to excuse me from the world temporarily, because I want to be OK with my existence in the world, just as I am. Whatever gay experience I thought I was missing out on, I've had it now. I've been there. Turns out, I don't like being there. And I think I'm done with it.

So, you're done with all that forever?

I can't give you a fairytale ending to this story. At least, not yet. All I can tell you for sure is that I'm trying to stop using meth. I'm trying to remind myself, even on my hardest days, that the high is temporary, the crash is brutal, and that the hard shit will still be there and harder than ever, unlike meth dick. I'm trying not to be the stereotype of the gay that's hooked on meth. I'm trying.

So, is the stereotype true?

Most gay men aren't getting drunk and doing drugs every weekend. While we are more likely to do drugs than straight people, we're not more likely to drink than them, just more likely to hang out at bars. So, it's not as true as you've been made to believe. However, we can't ignore that LGBTQ+ drink more and do more drugs than straight people. It's one of the challenges that comes along with being part of this marginalized community. Maybe it's because bars are our safe space. Maybe it's because we have more mental health challenges. Maybe it's because we're more likely to need an escape from a world that struggles to accept us. Whatever the cause, the stereotype is true, at least for the LGBTQ+ community as a whole.

What's the final verdict?

Mostly true.

SCORING YOUR QUIZ: QUESTION #16

In the quiz (page 14), we asked if you got drunk and/or did drugs last month. Here's how to score your results:

a. Got drunk only: 0 gay points (gays are just as likely as straights to drink)

b. Did drugs only: 1 gay point (gays are more likely than straights to do drugs)

c. Got drunk and did drugs: still just 1 gay point (because you don't get any bonus points for drinking)

d. None of the above: 0 gay points

17

You Probably Love Iced Coffee

What's the stereotype?

Gays love iced coffee.

Iced coffee? Really?

Yup. Whether you've heard of it or not, there's a newer stereotype that says that gays love iced coffee. Not just any coffee. Iced coffee. Whether it's in the summer or the winter, whether it will make us late to work or not, we would rather die than go without our iced coffee. Caffeine isn't the worst possible vice, but, according to the stereotype, we're hooked.

Kyle, you drink iced coffee, right?

The first coffee drink I ever ordered for myself was a Caramel Frappuccino. I was in high school, and I wanted to like coffee because so many of my classmates did. It seemed like the cool thing to do, liking coffee. But I didn't know where to start.

The girl I was dating at the time (lol) and I liked to walk around the Katy Mills Mall, a typical hangout spot for bored high schoolers. One of the times we were there, she took me to Starbucks and told me to try the Frappuccino. I did, and it was delicious. Thus, my affinity for iced coffee started when I was still in the closet.

When I moved to Seattle out of college for a full-time job, I figured I would need a more grown-up drink to match my new grown-up life. Caramel Frappuccinos seemed sophomoric to me now. That's when I made the switch over to vanilla lattes (yes, the hot kind of coffee). At some point, I decided those weren't adult enough and made the move to an americano with cream and sugar.

It was when I was dating my first real, long-term boyfriend that I learned about classic iced coffees. It was his go-to Starbucks order, and he ordered it all. the. time. I picked up on it, too, and started ordering them for myself, even after we broke up.

It wouldn't be for another several years until I came to understand that iced coffee was a gay stereotype. In looking it up, all signs point to 2018 as the year it became enough of a thing that articles were written about it on sites like BuzzFeed and Vice and LogoTV.com.

But why? What is it about iced coffee that makes it part of gay culture?

Several articles pointed out that Jack, the flamboyantly gay character from *Will & Grace,* had an affinity for iced coffee in an episode from 2001 (season 3, episode 11, if you must know). In it, Jack meets an attractive barista, so he orders iced coffee over and over and over again to satiate his thirst. According to Jack, "[the cute barista] gives me free iced coffee every time I go which is every hour on the hour." His obsession for iced coffee stems on the hotness of the employee, not the gayness of iced coffee itself, so it's probably not the original source of the 2018 emergence of this stereotype. However, it might be one of the first ways iced coffee was incepted into our brains as being a "gay thing," long before the association popped up on the internet.

Another media reference came in the major(ly) gay movie, 2018's *Love, Simon*. In it, the titular Simon says, "We do everything friends do: We drink way too much iced coffee, we watch bad 90s movies, and hang out at Waffle House dreaming of college and gorging on carbs." The 2018 timing seems to line up, but maybe *Love, Simon* was just echoing a growing theme that already existed on the internet: iced coffee is kinda gay.

I'm no internet sleuth, but with some basic searching on Google, one of the earliest references I can find online is from May 2018. It's a Tumblr post with a gif of Jack drinking an iced coffee from that very episode of *Will & Grace*. Below it is the caption: "Iced coffee: The official sponsor of the gay agenda." The gif was posted to—get this—the official Tumblr for *Will & Grace*. The new version of *Will & Grace* ran from 2017–2020, so maybe this was part of their attempts at viral marketing for the new show. Maybe they realized they had tapped into some gay stereotype long before the internet realized it to be true.

The very earliest reference I can find is from @KatDene who, in September 2017, tweeted, "Look I'm just a gay millennial trying to live my life, I don't need to worry about people judging my basic ass iced coffee drinks." Some of my other favorite iced coffee tweets:

- "gays are inherently stronger because of their iced coffee consumption" @visceramami on June 12, 2018
- "Iced coffee is a full gay meal" @mtehuitz on September 6, 2018
- "I think it's time us gays make it known that iced coffee is under OUR ownership and that if you have dipped [sic]/ are sipping/will sip iced coffee during pride month that you WILL turn gay" @omariospizza on June 20, 2018.

And there's a plethora of similar tweets out there pointing out the connection between being gay and iced coffee.

No matter exactly when it started, there seemed to be an explosion of articles about how gay iced coffee was in 2018 and 2019. In 2018, BuzzFeed posted an article called "This Post Will Only Make Sense If You're Gay and Love Iced Coffee." Also in 2018, LogoTV.com posted an article called, "ICED COFFEE AS GAY CULTURE: AN EXPLORATION." (Yes, it was in all caps. No, I don't know why they're yelling at me. Maybe they had too much iced coffee.) In 2019, *GQ* published an article called, "Why Is Iced Coffee So Gay?" where the last sentence reads: "Iced coffee gives queer people power. It is, to put it bluntly, gay as fuck."

Why is it gay as fuck, though?

Hold on, we'll get there soon enough. There's no shortage of discourse around iced coffee as part of the gay community. In their 2019 article, Vice posted about iced coffee calling it one of the "new gay stereotypes." Indeed, this stereotype is different than some of the other ones we've written about, like limp wrists (see Chapter 4) or ear piercings (see Chapter 3) which have been around for decades. This stereotype seems to have cropped up in the past five years or so. Other "new gay stereotypes" they mentioned include the fact that gays can't drive and that gays can't sit properly. I'd add to that list of new stereotypes that gays can't do math, a joke I've seen online for some time now.

The fact that new stereotypes are popping up serves as a reminder that they are socially constructed and continue to evolve over time. So why, then, iced coffee? Why not some other mundane object to pin an assumption of gayness to?

Some articles I read talked about how iced coffee is more of an urban thing. Unlike regular coffee, it's not something that's made at

home; it's something you'd walk to a coffee shop to purchase, especially if you're looking for cold brew. And anything associated with
the city is associated with gays because of the assumption that we
migrate to liberal cities where we can be more accepted. (Note: one
study says up to 20% of LGBTQ+ people live in urban areas, so the
idea of the liberal city gay is only part of the picture.[102])

Many of the articles I read also focused on the fact that iced
coffee was more "feminine" than hot. My first Frappuccino was
mostly sugar, covered in whipped cream and drizzled with caramel,
and conventional stereotypes say that women, more than men, like
their desserts. There was also a phase in the 2000s where female
celebrities were all seen drinking their iced coffee. Britney Spears
(and gifs of Britney Spears) came up multiple times as a female icon
who popularly expressed love for her iced coffee around this time.
Maybe this, like *Will & Grace,* was just one more time iced coffee
was incepted into our brains as being more feminine, which is often
similarly viewed as more gay. In addition, iced coffee is sometimes
more expensive than regular coffee, and extravagant purchases are
seen as a female interest.

Now, I suppose I have to talk about the straw, which iced coffee is
generally consumed from. Sure, there's the fact that drinking through
a straw is more bougie, and looking over your glasses at someone
while judging them is more satisfying if done while sipping on a
straw. Gays love anything that's a little bougie and a lot judgmental.
But, ultimately, the straw connection seems to be the obvious one that
gays have an oral fixation and love anything long and cylindrical. If
we have a choice of sipping through a cup or putting something in
our mouth and sucking on it, we'll always choose the latter.

OMG, I didn't even think about the sucking on a straw thing!

Another major theme that was a little more subtle than the "straw

= dick" discourse was the fact that iced coffee is counter-culture, especially during the cold winter months. In 2019, *Gay Star News* published an article featuring an image of a New Yorker walking outside through a blizzard, one hand grabbing onto the hood of his winter coat, and the other holding on to an iced coffee. The image had originally been tweeted by the official City of New York account. What *Gay Star News* picked up on is that, in the comments of the tweet, many people identified this as part of gay culture. While no one actually knew the sexual identity of the person in the picture, nor did he have any clear gay markings (other than his drink), assumptions and gay gifs were abound. "Iced coffee as a part of gay culture has been part of the lexicon for around two years," the article read,[103] helping inform those that were unaware of the stereotype why the gay publication would be discussing iced coffee at all. *GQ* even picked up on this in their 2019 article,[104] titled "Why Is Iced Coffee So Gay?" Being gay isn't as widely accepted as it should be. It's seen as going against the grain. Because of this, we have a penchant for things that, like ourselves, go against the grain. Iced coffee during winter has become one of those things. As user @yashar tweeted, "Neither snow nor rain nor heat nor gloom of night stays these homos from an iced coffee beverage." In the past, counter-culture might have meant getting tattoos or protesting the war. I think the fact that this is an accessible counter-culture activity is what makes it sticky. Most anyone can purchase iced coffee for a small amount of money and feel like they're in on the joke.

The articles I read provided plenty of other suggestions as to where this stereotype came from, including:

- it goes in cute cups that are very portable
- it's hip
- it's a vice, but one of the less-harmful vices to indulge in
- it's customizable.

Yes, all of those were included in various articles as possible explanations as to where the stereotype of gays loving iced coffee came from. Like I say when looking at a row of naked men, some of those are a bigger stretch than others.

While I don't know if we'll be able to pin down exactly where the stereotype came from, one reason I think this caught on is that gays like subtle ways to signal to other gays. We've talked about the hanky code and ear piercings (see Chapter 3). We appreciate (and sometimes need) to have those clues we can drop to hint out our sexual identity without actually coming out. Sometimes it's because it isn't safe. Sometimes it's a new environment where we need to test the waters. Other times, we just don't want to have to do the whole rigmarole that's included when coming out. Whatever the reason, having ways of signaling our gayness to each other, even when they're not definitive, is useful. I remember when I got my first full-time job at Microsoft and had to write an "about me" paragraph to be sent out to the team. I mentioned that I loved watching *Bravo* as my way of hinting that I was gay to those that were in the know without having to risk coming out to a brand-new group of people whose views on LGBTQ+ people I didn't know quite yet. Iced coffee is one of those, albeit new, signals that we now have in our toolkit that we can use to hint that we're gay.

And when you think about it, straight people have their stereotypical drinks, too. Take Monster Energy drink or Mountain Dew; these drinks are marketed to straight men and have a very straight appeal to them. Even though they have high sugar content, these are drinks that just "feel" straight. That's part of the problem of associating stereotypes of sexual orientation to any particular drink. So much of it is based on marketing and cultural assumptions that logic doesn't actually factor into it in any reasonable way. I associate Mountain Dew with gamers, but gays can be gaymers, too, so why is it so connected in my brain to straight men?

Really, I think iced coffee is a blank canvas that we've decided to paint gayness onto. It's a relatively generic, unobtrusive object that, in reality, has no gender or orientation. It isn't something that's pushed on us from a young age. There's nothing obscene or offensive about it. There isn't a lot of baggage that comes along with iced coffee. So, it's something we've found that we latched onto, and people on the internet snowballed it into a fun, lighthearted joke.

But is it really lighthearted?

Given its banality, it's interesting to look at this stereotype and ask if it's good, bad, or neutral. Is the act of creating stereotypes, in and of itself, harmful? In an article on *i-D*,[105] author Brian O'Flynn writes, "Why does it irritate me so much to be told I enjoy a frozen beverage when I don't (particularly)?" For those that may not like iced coffee, stereotypes may not be in good fun; they might feel, as Flynn describes it, "grating, perhaps even alienating." Because this stereotype doesn't have any solid basis that I could discover, it means some group of people will be excluded from it, whether that's because they dislike iced coffee or because they're unaware the stereotype even exists.

I also think gays tend to weaponize stereotypes, no matter how big or small. I remember when I told a fellow gay that I had never seen *Steel Magnolias*, he called me "deficient." We have a tendency to take the expectations we have of gay people, no matter where they came from, and project them on to others. If they don't meet that projected expectation, we think there's something wrong with that person. How many times have you heard the phrase, "I should take away your gay card!" because you haven't seen some movie or don't like some pop artist or don't know of some celebrity. And it happens with iced coffee, too. User @tt3rb tweeted, "Are you even gay if stopping to get iced coffee doesn't make you late to work."

There's also the (very meta) argument that iced coffee as a stereotype serves to poke fun at the very idea of gay stereotypes. In the *i-D* article, O'Flynn interviewed a Twitter user, Mike Dolan, who said that, "It's a satirisation and exaggeration of the process we went through being told that certain character traits and ways of expressing ourselves were gay." Maybe we're so used to stereotypes being handed down to us from generations ago, and we collectively, if not subconsciously, decided to create our own as a way to take back control of the narrative. If we create the stereotype, we can't be insulted by it if it's hurled against us.

For better or worse, the stereotype that gays drink iced coffee exists. As someone who is fascinated by where stereotypes come from and why, this one is particularly interesting because it's part of a new wave of stereotypes that has only existed for a handful of years, fueled by the internet. It's built on shaky footing, but it's a reminder that gay culture continues to evolve, and new stereotypes will continue to be created. Stereotypes aren't edicts sent from above; rather they're socially created, and new ones will continue to spring up.

Unlike stereotypes of the past, this one is far more innocuous than, say, the idea that we're crazy or that we're pedophiles. I think the gay community has more agency now than it did in the past, and rather than being the target of stereotyping that others did against us, we get to create our own. And, given that opportunity to create our own stereotypes, we decided that iced coffee is gay. Nowadays, I don't always order an iced coffee, but when I do, I feel extra gay, even if there isn't any logical reason behind it.

So, is the stereotype true?

Based on what the internet says, iced coffee is definitively gay culture, starting around 2017. For some people, it rings true. For others, it's a frustrating new stereotype that makes them feel excluded. The exact source of the stereotype is hard to pin down. Some theories are that it's urban, it's more feminine, or even that it's phallic. Some point to *Will & Grace* as the original source of the stereotype. No matter where it came from, this stereotype doesn't have any solid footing to stand on. In spite of the many attempts to explain where this one came from, there's no definitive proof that says gays are more likely to drink iced coffee. It seems this one was invented by the internet and locked into our consciousness from there.

What's the final verdict?

False.

SCORING YOUR QUIZ: QUESTION #17

In the quiz (page 14), we asked how often you drink iced coffee. Here's how to score your results:

- **a.** Never: 0 gay points
- **b.** Sometimes: 0 gay points
- **c.** Every day and twice on Sundays: 0 gay points
- **d.** Only when Taylor the latte boy is working: 1 gay point

QUIZ   SCORING YOUR QUIZ

1. a=2, b=0, c=1, d=1
2. a=0, b=1, c=2, d=3
3. a=0, b=2, c=1
4. a=2, b=2, c=0, d=-1
5. a=0, b=0, c=0
6. a=2, b=1, c=0, d=5
7. a=2, b=1, c=0
8. a=-1, b=0, c=1, d=0
9. a=0, b=1, c=2, d=5

10. a=2, b=2, c=2, d=2, e=0
11. a=0, b=0, c=0, d=0
12. a=2, b=1, c=0, d=-1
13. a=2, b=1, c=0, d=-1
14. a=0, b=0, c=-1
15. a=0, b=2, c=5
16. a=0, b=1, c=1, d=0
17. a=0, b=0, c=0, d=1

If you scored...

-5 to 0   You're Ron Swanson, a real heterosexual dude's dude.

1 to 10   You're Ken (as played by Ryan Gosling), a straight dude with some big feelings.

11 to 20   You're Simon from Love, Simon, a kinda straight-washed version of a gay.*

21 to 30   You're Stanford Blatch from Sex and the City, clearly a homo but buttoned-up.**

30 to 35   You're Jack McFarlane, and you already know who that is.

....

* And you're in the same category as Mike, who scored a 14.
** And you're in the same category as Kyle, who scored a 21.

Conclusion
You're Probably Gayish

You've arrived at the end of the book! Congrats! We knew you could do it! By now, you've filled out the quiz, gotten a score, and read through all the reasons why we're pretty sure you're at least a little bit Gayish. Now, just like the podcast, we're going to do our Gayest and Straightest, but first...

When we started out writing this book and outlining what chapters we thought we were going to include, both of us thought that more of these were going to be false. We're always picking apart different stereotypes on the podcast, and although a lot of them are based on some grain of truth, more often than not it feels like a bit of a stretch to say that they are true. It doesn't really matter if they're true or not. There is no wrong way to be gay. If you get nothing else out of reading this book, we hope it is this very core of what we set out to do when starting the podcast all those years ago: There is no wrong way to be gay.

At the end of every episode of the podcast, we do our "Gayest and Straightest." It is the stereotypically gayest and stereotypically straightest thing about us that week. When we have guests they usually give us theirs as well, and we very often play our listeners' offerings they leave us on our hotline (standard rates apply). The segment is meant to show that everyone has a little of column A and a little of column B all the time, even straight people. We have gotten a little bit of flak for including the segment. Some people don't seem to understand that we're trying to poke fun at stereotypes.

The secrets to picking good stereotypes for our Straightest each week are basically anything to do, no matter how vaguely, with traditionally masculine gender roles. Think changing a tire, or going hunting. Watching or playing sports are pretty straight. Not caring about personal appearance or hygiene can be a good source. Being mistaken for straight, especially by interested straight women, is a winner.

As for our Gayest each week, like we've seen in this book a few times there is a connection between the perception that someone is gay and things we consider to be feminine. Going shopping, listening to pop divas, drinking iced coffee... a lot of the stereotypes that became chapters of this book have been good candidates to draw on. Basically anything that toxically masculine culture would do and then feel compelled to say "but no homo" afterwards.

Stereotypes, especially those that come up as we discuss our Gayest and Straightest each week, rely on antiquated rules about gender roles. So, to make it very clear: gender is a construct. For all of the breathless screaming from the right in the US that "THERE ARE ONLY TWO GENDERS, PERIOD," they're factually incorrect. They're like Don Quixote pretending windmills are giants and feeling noble for fighting them. Whether gender expression and traditionally masculine and feminine roles have value or are based in an objective truth or not, gender expression is not sexual orientation. Once more, for the windmill screamers at the back: GENDER EXPRESSION IS NOT SEXUAL ORIENTATION.

The next time you see someone do something and you think you know something about their sexual orientation, you might be right. You also might be very wrong. Act accordingly.

Writing a book takes a very long time, so we're going to do our Gayest and Straightest of the last seven years or so as we sign off.

What is Kyle's Gayest and Straightest?

My Straightest is the fact that I've never seen the movie *Steel Magnolias.* (Sorry, Dolly.) When I brought up this fact to a gay acquaintance over drinks, his immediate response was to call me "deficient" and act aghast at my very existence. Sure, maybe it's a good movie. Maybe it's a movie I should watch sometime. But my media consumption is my own choosing, and the fact that I haven't seen this one film doesn't make me any less than. This was one of those moments that helped inspire the podcast because I wanted a place to talk about all the ways that we're made to feel "deficient" as gay men, even by those within the community.

My Gayest is my perpetual and unwavering love for Britney. Even now as she twirls on her Instagram videos, I love her. Her music makes me happy. It's upbeat and catchy and sometimes slutty and fun and puts me in a good mood. Sometimes, I'll wear my Britney t-shirt, a skirt, and my black sparkly flats, and it's the gayest outfit I've ever worn. She enriches my life (and wardrobe) in a wonderful, gay way.

What is Mike's Gayest and Straightest?

My Straightest is my continuing love of drinking beer. I don't always get to, since keto is my go-to for losing weight and beer on keto is a no-no. But anytime I take a little break from my diet, I go back to beer. Quite specifically I prefer the most watered down light beer available, and I have my favorite local version picked out for almost everywhere I go. Beer is so quintessentially straight guy, in my opinion, I put it in our theme song.

My Gayest has been my search for the ten inch penis. I don't believe they exist, and I have said so on the show many many times. Usually we say that sex doesn't count, since that's less a stereotype of being gay and more an expression of actual gayness. But being a size queen is a gay stereotype, and one I'm getting more and more comfortable admitting applies to me. Also talking about dicks, whether for sex purposes or not, is just part of having gay friends. One side bonus has been the number of men, some quite well endowed, that have reached out to me to start a conversation, usually some variation of "I'm not ten inches, but..." Some of those chats have led to some pretty steamy places and even a couple of friendships. Another side bonus has been all of the pictures of dicks that have been sent to me to prove me wrong. Every single one has been either fake, or not really ten inches. The quest continues.

Thank you for reading; we hope you learned something. That's it! This has been *You're Probably Gayish*. Until next book: Be butch, be fabulous, be you! (See you next week.)

Endnotes

1   Drescher, J. (2015) "Out of DSM: Depathologizing homosexuality." *Behavioral Sciences, 5*(4), 565–575. www.ncbi.nlm.nih.gov/pmc/articles/PMC4695779

2   Wikimedia Foundation (2024) Sigmund Freud's views on homosexuality. Wikipedia. https://en.wikipedia.org/wiki/Sigmund_Freud%27s_views_on_homosexuality

3   National Alliance on Mental Illness (2024) *LGBTQ+*. NAMI. www.nami.org/your-journey/identity-and-cultural-dimensions/lgbtq

4   Heilmann, A., & Llewellyn, M. (2014) "The Victorians, Sex, and Gender." *The Oxford Handbook of Victorian Literary Culture*, 161–177. Oxford University Press.

5   American Psychological Association. (n.d.). Former APA presidents. American Psychological Association. www.apa.org/about/governance/president/former-presidents

6   Bullough, V.L., & Voght, M. (1978) "Homosexuality Part III and its confusion with the 'Secret Sin' in pre-Freudian America." *GALA Review, 1*(8), 16+.

7   Pocock, J. (2015) "Not so lonely: Busting the myth of the only child." *JSTOR Daily Education & Society*, November 18. https://daily.jstor.org/myth-lonely-only-child

8   Polit, D.F., & Falbo, T. (1987) "Only children and personality development: A quantitative review." *Journal of Marriage and Family, 49*(2), 309–325.

9   Nguyen, C. (2017, April 13) "A linkage between DNA markers on the X chromosome and male sexual orientation." Embryo Project Encyclopedia, April 13. https://hdl.handle.net/10776/11476

10 Hamer, D.H., Hu, S., Magnuson, V.L., Hu, N., & Pattatucci, A.M. (1993) "A linkage between DNA markers on the X chromosome and male sexual orientation." *Science, 261*, 321–327.

11 Rice, G., Anderson, C., Risch, N., & Ebers, G. (1999) "Male homosexuality: Absence of linkage to Microsatellite markers at Xq28." *Science, 284*(5414), 665–667.

12 Lehmiller, J. (2020) "Why do some identical twins have different sexual orientations?" Kinsey Institute Research & Institute News, June 25. https://blogs.iu.edu/kinseyinstitute/2020/06/25/why-do-some-identical-twins-have-different-sexual-orientations

13   Ganna, A., Verweij, K.J.H., Nivard, M.G., Maier, R., et al. (2019) "No 'gay gene':
     Massive study homes in on genetic basis of human sexuality." *Science, 365*(6456),
     869–873.

14   Blanchard, R. (2001) "Fraternal birth order and the maternal immune hypothesis of
     male homosexuality." *Hormones and Behavior, 40*(2), 105–114.

15   Blanchard, R., Krupp, J., VanderLaan, D.P., Vasey, P.L., & Zucker, K.J. (2020) "A
     method yielding comparable estimates of the fraternal birth order and fe-
     male fecundity effects in male homosexuality." *Proceedings of the Royal
     Society B,* 28720192907. https://royalsocietypublishing.org/doi/full/10.1098/
     rspb.2019.2907?af=R&

16   Berlinger, M. (2019) "Why men are embracing the single dangly earring." *The
     New York Times,* November 12. www.nytimes.com/2019/11/12/fashion/mens-single-
     dangly-earring.html

17   Horne, J., Knox, D., Zusman, J., & Zusman, M.E. (2007) "Tattoos and piercings: Atti-
     tudes, behaviors, and interpretations of college students." *College Student Journal,
     41*(4). https://go.gale.com/ps/i.do?id=GALE%7CA172977998&sid=googleScholar&v=2
     .1&it=r&linkaccess=abs&issn=01463934&p=AONE&sw=w&userGroupName=anon%7
     Ee02a9c54

18   The Cultural Heritage of India (Vol-II): The Ramkrishna Mission Institute of Culture
     Calcutta. Internet Archive (1970). https://archive.org/details/in.ernet.dli.2015.185512/
     page/n7/mode/2up

19   Steele, V. (ed.) (2015) *The Berg Companion to Fashion.* Bloomsbury.

20   DeMello, M. (2007) *Encyclopedia of Body Adornment.* Greenwood Press.

21   Lyons, D.C. (1989) "The earring thing." *Ebony,* January, 98–100. https://indexarticles.
     com/reference/ebony/the-earring-thing-more-men-now-wearing-earrings

22   Napolitano, N. (2012) 'Left is right, right is wrong:' An examination of body
     piercing, deviant subculture, and contemporary connotations." *The Point Journal,
     61.* https://thepointjournal.org/2012/12/07/point-61-left-is-right-right-is-wrong-
     an-examination-of-body-piercing-deviant-subculture-and-contemporary-
     connotations

23   Fischer, H. (2015) *Gay Semiotics.* Cherry and Martin.

24   Editors (2024) "Which ear is the gay ear? Unpacking this dated stereotype."
     Queerty, January 29. www.queerty.com/brief-history-signaling-gay-ear-
     myth-20220130

25   Hall, T. (1991) "Piercing fad is turning convention on its ear." *The New York Times,*
     May 19.

26   Wikimedia Foundation (2023) Recurring Saturday night live characters and sketches
     introduced 1989–90. Wikipedia. https://en.wikipedia.org/wiki/Recurring_Saturday_
     Night_Live_characters_and_sketches_introduced_1989%E2%80%9390#Lyle_the_
     Effeminate_Heterosexual

27   Anderson, V. (Dir.) (1956) Tea and Sympathy [Film]. Metro-Goldwyn-Mayer (MGM).

28   King, T.A. (2004) *The Gendering of Men, 1600–1750, Vol. 2.* Madison, W: IUniversity
     of Wisconsin Press.

29   Chauncey, G. (2005) *Gay New York: Gender, Urban Culture, and the Making of the
     Gay Male World, 1890–1940.* Basic Books.

30   McDonnell, M.A. (2006) *Roman Manliness: Virtus and the Roman Republic.* Cam-
     bridge University Press.

31 Johnson, K.L., Gill, S., Reichman, V., & Tassinary, L.G. (2007) "Swagger, sway, and sexuality: Judging sexual orientation from body motion and morphology." *Journal of Personality and Social Psychology, 93*(3), 321–334.

32 Innala, S.M., & Ernulf, K.E. (1994) "When gay is pretty: Physical attractiveness and low homophobia." *Psychological Reports, 74*(3 Pt 1), 827–831.

33 Proto, D. (2022) "Gay men push back on body shaming amid high rates of body dysmorphia, eating disorders." Good Morning America, June 28. www.goodmorningamerica.com/wellness/story/gay-men-push-back-body-shaming-amid-high-85406736

34 Peplau, L.A., Frederick, D.A., Yee, C., Maisel, N., Lever, J., & Ghavami, N. (2008) "Body image satisfaction in heterosexual, gay, and lesbian adults." *Archives of Sexual Behavior, 38*(5), 713–725. https://link.springer.com/article/10.1007/s10508-008-9378-1

35 Yelland, C., & Tiggemann, M. (2003) "Muscularity and the gay ideal: Body dissatisfaction and disordered eating in homosexual men." *Eating Behaviors, 4*(2), 107–116. https://pubmed.ncbi.nlm.nih.gov/15000974

36 Carroll, L. (2010) "Gay guys really are thinner, study says." NBCNews.com, June 8. www.nbcnews.com/health/health-news/gay-guys-really-are-thinner-study-says-flna1c9446808

37 Tedder, R. (2024) "Why are gay men thinner than hetero guys (and lesbians fatter than straight girls)?" Queerty, January 29. www.queerty.com/why-are-gay-men-thinner-than-hetero-guys-and-lesbians-fatter-than-straight-girls-20100608

38 Kane, G.D. (2010) "Revisiting gay men's body image issues: Exposing the fault lines." *Review of General Psychology, 14*(4), 311–317.

39 Yelland, C., & Tiggemann, M. (2003) "Muscularity and the gay ideal: Body dissatisfaction and disordered eating in homosexual men." *Eating Behaviors, 4*(2), 107–116. https://pubmed.ncbi.nlm.nih.gov/15000974

40 Martin, J.T., & Nguyen, D.H. (2004) "Anthropometric analysis of homosexuals and heterosexuals: Implications for early hormone exposure." *Hormones and Behavior, 45*(1), 31–39.

41 Hughes, S.M., & Bremme, R. (2011) "The effects of facial symmetry and sexually-dimorphic facial proportions on assessments of sexual orientation." *Journal of Social, Evolutionary, and Cultural Psychology, 5*(4), 214–230.

42 Valentova, J.V., Kleisner, K., Havlíček, J., & Neustupa, J. (2014) "Shape differences between the faces of homosexual and heterosexual men." *Archives of Sexual Behavior, 43*(2), 353–361.

43 Reid, J. (1977) *The Best Little Boy in the World.* New York: Ballantine Books.

44 Pachankis, J.E., & Hatzenbuehler, M.L. (2013) "The social development of contingent self-worth in sexual minority young men: An empirical investigation of the 'best little boy in the world' hypothesis." *Basic and Applied Social Psychology, 35*(2), 176–190.

45 Sansone, D. (2019) "LGBT students: New evidence on demographics and educational outcomes." *Economics of Education Review, 73*, 1019331.

46 Dorris, J. (2022) "A world of pride: Gay designers talk about acceptance and challenges." *Interior Design*, November 18. https://interiordesign.net/designwire/a-world-of-pride-gay-designers-talk-about-acceptance-and-challenges

47 Zippia (n.d.) "Commercial interior designer demographics and statistics in the US." www.zippia.com/commercial-interior-designer-jobs/demographics

48   Jones, J.M. (2024) "LGBT identification in U.S. ticks up to 7.1%." Gallup.com. https://news.gallup.com/poll/389792/lgbt-identification-ticks-up.aspx

49   Matthews, C., & Hill, C. (2011) "Gay until proven straight: Exploring perceptions of male interior designers from male practitioner and student perspectives." *Journal of Interior Design, 36*(3), 15–34.

50   Murphy, R. (2023) "Gay men, it's time to let ourselves be slobs." Slate Magazine. https://slate.com/human-interest/2023/06/gay-stereotypes-where-did-it-come-from-and-how-do-we-beat-it.html

51   Suckling, L. (2017) "Not all gay men are interiors experts." Stuff. www.stuff.co.nz/life-style/homed/decor/95603828/not-all-gay-men-are-interiors-experts

52   Lusher, A. (2016) "Stereotyping gay men as stylish and witty 'prevents people seeing them as proper individuals'." *The Independent*, February 9. www.independent.co.uk/news/people/stereotyping-gay-men-as-stylish-and-witty-prevents-people-seeing-them-as-proper-individuals-a6861296.html

53   Givhan, R. (2013) "New York fashion exhibit examines the influence of gay designers." *The Washington Post*, September 17.

54   ABC News (2006) "Gay stereotypes: Are they true?" https://abcnews.go.com/2020/story?id=2449185&page=1

55   Cotner, C., & Burkley, M. (2013) "Queer eye for the straight guy: Sexual orientation and stereotype lift effects on performance in the fashion domain." *Journal of Homosexuality, 60*(9), 1336–1348.

56   Wikimedia Foundation (2024) Lavender scare. Wikipedia. https://en.wikipedia.org/wiki/Lavender_Scare

57   Eugenios, J. (2022) "How 1970s Christian crusader Anita Bryant helped spawn Florida's LGBTQ culture war." NBCNews.com, April 13. www.nbcnews.com/nbc-out/out-news/1970s-christian-crusader-anita-bryant-helped-spawn-floridas-lgbtq-cult-rcna24215

58   Wikimedia Foundation (2024) Florida Legislative Investigation Committee. Wikipedia. https://en.wikipedia.org/wiki/Florida_Legislative_Investigation_Committee

59   Herek, G.M. (n.d.) "Facts about homosexuality and child molestation." https://lgbpsychology.org/html/facts_molestation.html

60   Eugenios, J. (2022) "How 1970s Christian crusader Anita Bryant helped spawn Florida's LGBTQ culture war." NBCNews.com, April 13. www.nbcnews.com/nbc-out/out-news/1970s-christian-crusader-anita-bryant-helped-spawn-floridas-lgbtq-cult-rcna24215

61   Groth, A.N., & Birnbaum, H.J. (1978) "Adult sexual orientation and attraction to underage persons." *Archives of Sexual Behavior, 7*(3), 175–181.

62   Erickson, W.D., Walbek, N.H., & Seely, R.K. (1988) "Behavior patterns of child molesters." *Archives of Sexual Behavior, 17*(1), 77–86.

63   Herek, G.M. (n.d.) Gregory M. Herek, Ph.D. Biographical sketch of Gregory M. Herek. https://lgbpsychology.org/html/bio.html

64   Freund, K., Watson, R., & Rienzo, D. (1989) "Heterosexuality, homosexuality, and erotic age preference." *The Journal of Sex Research, 26*(1), 107–117.

65   Jenny, C., Roesler, T.A., & Poyer, K.L. (1994) "Are children at risk for sexual abuse by homosexuals?" *Pediatrics, 94*(1), 41–44.

66   American Psychological Association (n.d.) "Lesbian and gay parenting." American Psychological Association. www.apa.org/pi/lgbt/resources/parenting

67   Fox, T.C. (2009) "Study: No link between gay priests and sex abuse scandal." *National Catholic Reporter,* November 19. www.ncronline.org/blogs/ncr-today/study-no-link-between-gay-priests-and-sex-abuse-scandal

68   Herek, G. M. (n.d.) "Facts about homosexuality and child molestation." https://lgbpsychology.org/html/facts_molestation.html

69   RAINN (2020) "Grooming: Know the warning signs." www.rainn.org/news/grooming-know-warning-signs

70   Facebook (2023) www.facebook.com/groups/gayishpodcast/permalink/3969078799979705

71   Ellis, H. (2004) *The Project Gutenberg eBook of Studies in the Psychology of Sex, volume 2 (of 6), by Havelock Ellis.* Project Gutenberg. www.gutenberg.org/files/13611/13611-h/13611-h.htm

72   Wikimedia Foundation. (2024) Havelock Ellis. Wikipedia. https://en.wikipedia.org/wiki/Havelock_Ellis

73   Tilcsik, A., Anteby, M., & Knight, C.R. (2015) "Concealable stigma and occupational segregation: Toward a theory of gay and lesbian occupations." *Administrative Science Quarterly, 60*(3), 446–481.

74   Heslin, K., & Alfier, J. (2022) Sexual Orientation Differences in Access to Care and Health Status, Behaviors, and Beliefs: Findings from the National Health and Nutrition Examination Survey, National Survey of Family Growth, and National Health Interview Survey. www.cdc.gov/nchs/data/nhsr/nhsr171.pdf

75   Herek, G.M. (2002) "Heterosexuals' attitudes toward bisexual men and women in the United States." *The Journal of Sex Research, 39*(4), 264–274. www.jstor.org/stable/3813227

76   Attitude Magazine (2017) "Why do gay men love divas?" *Attitude,* September 7. www.attitude.co.uk/uncategorised/why-do-gay-men-love-divas-289113

77   Moughalabie, R.B. (2020) "Female pop diva adoration: Fandom in the gay community." https://thesis.eur.nl/pub/55213/Bou-Moughalabie-Ramzy.pdf

78   Jennex, C. (2013) "Diva worship and the sonic search for queer utopia." *Popular Music and Society, 36*(3), 343–359.

79   Ruitang, B.A. (2016) "Why are gay men so obsessed with Divas?" Medium. https://medium.com/@bobyandika/why-are-gay-men-so-obsessed-with-divas-ee4b6a9ef5e9

80   Out in Jersey (2022) "The music industry depends on the LGBTQ audience in surprising ways." https://outinjersey.net/the-music-industry-depends-on-the-lgbtq-audience-in-surprising-ways

81   Aronoff, U., & Gilboa, A. (2014) "Music and the closet: The roles music plays for gay men in the 'Coming out' process." *Psychology of Music, 43*(3), 423–437.

82   Draper, J. (2017) "'What has she actually *done*??!': Gay men, diva worship, and the paratextualization of gay-rights support." *Critical Studies in Media Communication, 34*(2), 130–137.

83   YouTube (2011) Neil Patrick Harris' 2011 Tony Awards opening number. YouTube. www.youtube.com/watch?v=-6S5caRGpK4

84   Healy, P. (2014) "In Broadway seats, few guys among the dolls." *The New York Times,* March 30. www.nytimes.com/2014/03/30/theater/in-broadway-seats-few-guys-among-the-dolls.html

85   Gimble, M. (Character) (2022) Schmigadoon! (TV series). www.tvfanatic.com/
     quotes/what-happens-when-youre-too-emotional-to-dance-does-it-loop-back
86   Zippia (2024) "Actor demographics and statistics [2024]: Number of actors in the
     US." www.zippia.com/actor-jobs/demographics
87   Bahr, S. (2020) "White actors and directors still dominate Broadway stages, report
     finds." *New York Times*, October 1. www.nytimes.com/2020/10/01/theater/new-york-
     theater-diversity-report.html
88   The Asian American Performers Action Coalition (n.d.) "The visibility report." www.
     aapacnyc.org/uploads/1/3/5/7/135720209/aapac_report_2018-2019_final.pdf www.
     aapacnyc.org/2018-2019.html
89   Scutti, S. (2017) "Gaydar: Why stereotypes matter when it comes to sexual orienta-
     tion." CNN, March 24. https://www.cnn.com/2017/03/24/health/gaydar-stereotypes-
     partner/index.html
90   Rule, N.O. (2017) "Perceptions of sexual orientation from minimal cues." *Archives of
     Sexual Behavior, 46*(1), 129–139.
91   Wikimedia Foundation (2024) "Demisexuality." Wikipedia. https://en.wikipedia.org/
     wiki/Demisexuality
92   Taylor, J.H. (1950) "The text of Augustine's De Genesi Ad Litteram." *Speculum, 25*(1),
     87–93.
93   Badcock, C. (2017) "It's the mode for men to have more sex partners." *Psychology
     Today*. www.psychologytoday.com/intl/blog/the-imprinted-brain/201703/it-s-the-
     mode-men-have-more-sex-partners
94   Bell, A.P., & Weinberg, M.S. (1978) *Homosexualities: A Study of Diversity Among
     Men and Women.* The Macmillan Company of Australia.
95   Van de Ven, P., Rodden, P., Crawford, J., & Kippax, S. (1997) "A comparative demo-
     graphic and sexual profile of older homosexually active men." *The Journal of Sex
     Research.* www.jstor.org/stable/3813472
96   Levin, E.M., Koopman, J.S., Aral, S.O., Holmes, K.K., & Foxman, B. (2009) "Charac-
     teristics of men who have sex with men and women and women who have sex with
     women and men: Results from the 2003 Seattle Sex Survey." *Sexually Transmitted
     Diseases, 36*(9), 541–546.
97   Trocki, K.F., Drabble, L., & Midanik, L. (2005) "Use of heavier drinking contexts
     among heterosexuals, homosexuals and bisexuals: Results from a National House-
     hold Probability Survey." *Journal of Studies on Alcohol and Drugs, 66*(1), 105–110.
98   Medley, G., Lipari, R.N., Bose, J., Cribb, D.S., Kroutil, L.A., & McHenry, G. (2016)
     "Sexual orientation and estimates of adult substance use and mental health:
     Results from the 2015 National Survey on Drug Use and Health." NSDUH Data
     Review. www.samhsa.gov/data/sites/default/files/NSDUH-SexualOrientation-2015/
     NSDUH-SexualOrientation-2015/NSDUH-SexualOrientation-2015.htm
99   McCabe, S.E., Hughes, T.L., Bostwick, W.B., West, B.T., & Boyd, C.J. (2009) "Sexual
     orientation, substance use behaviors and substance dependence in the United
     States." *Addiction (Abingdon, England), 104*(8), 1333–1345.
100 Hughes, T.L., Wilsnack, S.C., & Kantor, L.W. (2016) "The influence of gender and
     sexual orientation on alcohol use and alcohol-related problems: Toward a global
     perspective." *Alcohol Research: Current Reviews, 38*(1), 121–132.
101 Gilbert, P.A., Pass, L.E., Keuroghlian, A.S., Greenfield, T.K., & Reisner, S.L. (2018)
     "Alcohol research with transgender populations: A systematic review and

recommendations to strengthen future studies." *Drug and Alcohol Dependence*, *186*, 138–146.

102 Fadel, L. (2019) "LGBT people are a fundamental part of the fabric of rural commu-nities." NPR. www.npr.org/2019/04/04/709601295/lgbt-people-are-a-fundamental-part-of-the-fabric-of-rural-communities

103 Morgan, J. (2019) "Polar vortex is not deterring gay New Yorkers from drinking iced coffee." *Gay Star News*. www.gaystarnews.com/article/polar-vortex-did-not-deter-this-gay-new-yorker-from-drinking-iced-coffee

104 Kheraj, A. (2019) "Why is iced coffee so gay?" *GQ*, April 30. www.gq.com/story/iced-coffee-gay-rights

105 O'Flynn, B. (2019) "Why are we suddenly claiming everything is queer?" *i-D*, July 18. https://i-d.vice.com/en/article/bj9q5d/new-gay-stereotypes-iced-coffee